COLLINS
COBUILD

PHRASAL VERBS WORKBOOK

Malcolm Goodale

HarperCollins*Publishers*

HarperCollins Publishers
77-85 Fulham Palace Road
London W6 8JB

COBUILD is a trademark of William Collins Sons & Co Ltd

© HarperCollins Publishers Ltd 1993
First published 1993

10 9 8 7 6 5 4 3 2 1

The author is a teacher at the United Nations in Geneva.
The views expressed herein are those of the author and do not
necessarily reflect the views of the United Nations.

ISBN 0 00 370925 6

Design and typesetting by
eMC Design, 2 Grange Lane, Bromham,
Bedfordshire MK43 8NP

Printed and bound in Great Britain by
M & A Thomson Litho Ltd, Glasgow

Acknowledgements

The author and publisher would like to thank Katy Shaw for
her valuable comments on the manuscript.

The author and publishers are grateful to Punch Library
Services for permission to reproduce the cartoons in this book.

The publishers would like to thank those authors and publishers
who kindly gave permission for copyright material to be used in
the Bank of English, from which the examples in this book have
been taken.

Author's Note

This one is for Joanna and Steven.

My thanks go to:

Kamuran and Murat for putting up with me, Chen and my
students for trying the book out, Jean-Noel and Susan for
looking it over, and Annette for being there to fall back on.

CONTENTS

INTRODUCTION

This workbook accompanies the Collins COBUILD Dictionary of Phrasal Verbs. Though the workbook can be used on its own, more benefit will be gained by working closely with the Dictionary. Practice is approached through the individual particles, as featured in the Particles Index of the Dictionary.

The Collins COBUILD Dictionary of Phrasal Verbs lists over 3,000 phrasal verbs and explains over 5,500 different meanings. This workbook practises the most important phrasal verbs, with around 300 different meanings. Almost 50% of these are formed with 18 common verbs. Six common verbs - *bring, come, get, go, put* and *take* - account for nearly 30% of the phrasal verbs in this workbook.

This workbook is a vocabulary book rather than a grammar book. The examples and exercises throughout the book show the different syntactic patterns of the phrasal verbs. Whilst working on this book, it was found that the most important phrasal verbs are nearly always adverbial. These are also the most difficult phrasal verbs for learners to understand. It is for this reason that prepositional phrasal verbs are not included in this workbook.

For a detailed explanation of the grammar of phrasal verbs please refer to the Collins Cobuild English Grammar, as well as the introduction in the Collins Cobuild Dictionary of Phrasal Verbs.

HOW TO USE THE WORKBOOK

There are ten units of material. The first nine units deal with single particles and these units are arranged in alphabetical sequence in the book; the final unit concentrates on seven more particles. All the units follow a similar format, and can be studied in any order. As this book is designed both for classwork and self-study, an answer key to the exercises is given at the back of the book.

Every unit has an introductory page giving the important meanings of the particle being studied, with lists of the phrasal verbs to be practised in each section of the unit. Sometimes a phrasal verb appears twice in the same section, with two meanings. Quite often, a phrasal verb appears in two or three different sections. This is not surprising, as most phrasal verbs have more than one meaning, and can sometimes have as many as 20 different meanings.

The final section of each unit is called Other Meanings. This includes phrasal verbs which often do fit into a category of meaning, but the category is too small or too limited in its meaning to be included in this workbook. You will, of course, find them in the Particles Index of the Dictionary. The other phrasal verbs included in the

Other Meanings are those which are too common to be excluded, but which do not clearly fit into any particular category of meaning.

Under each category of meaning on the introductory page, space has been provided for other phrasal verbs to be added.

The Sections

Each section of a unit covers one category of meaning. If more than ten phrasal verbs are to be studied, the section is split into two parts. A section begins with example sentences, showing typical use of the phrasal verbs. The examples are often followed by Language Comments, which highlight other phrasal verbs with similar or opposite meanings, and which also give more formal equivalent verbs, when they exist. It is a common misconception that phrasal verbs are mostly used in spoken language. They can be found in many styles of writing, including highly formal government reports.

The Exercises

If a category of meaning includes phrasal verbs which are particularly difficult to understand, the first exercise asks you to complete the definitions of some or all of the phrasal verbs. Subsequent exercises involve matching phrases or sentences; choosing the phrasal verb that best fits a gapped sentence, from three alternatives provided; deciding on an appropriate phrasal verb to fill a gap, where no alternatives are given. For this last exercise you should pay particular attention to the form of the verb. Throughout the book you will also find exercises called Bad Jokes, where you are asked to match the two halves of the jokes.

In most sections, there is a final memorization exercise, which has an elephant symbol beside it. Memory is aided by links, connections, and images. We remember unusual things much more easily than 'normal' things. In this exercise you should write a paragraph containing at least one example of each of the phrasal verbs in the section you have just studied. The phrasal verbs do not necessarily have to be in the same order. You must use a minimum of words or images. It is very important to have a clear mental picture of your story; you should be able to see it as a little film in your head. To be more memorable, your paragraph could be exaggerated, strange, ridiculous, impossible, or amusing. The Answer Key contains a sample paragraph on page 140.

At the end of each unit there is a separate section of revision exercises, so that you can check your progress.

Enjoy using the Collins COBUILD Phrasal Verbs Workbook!

AWAY

Below are the two most important meanings of AWAY and one group of other meanings. In all 16 phrasal verbs have been selected.

Under each of the headings you will see a list of the phrasal verbs which you are going to practise. Some verbs appear more than once, as many phrasal verbs have more than one meaning.

You can write other phrasal verbs with the same meaning in the space provided. Use a dictionary if necessary.

A Withdrawing and Separating

break away
get away
give away
keep away
run away
take away

B Disappearing and Making things disappear

do away with
explain away
fade away
pass away
throw away

C Other meanings

get away with
hide away
put away
work away
write away

....

....

....

....

....

....

....

....

....

....

A Withdrawing and Separating

**break away   get away   give away
keep away   run away   take away**

*Two United Party senators broke away
to form the Federal Party.*

*His father had thought it would be good
for his character to get away from home
and earn some money on his own.*

*I could not decide whether to keep the
money he left me or give it away.*

*It would be better to keep away and not
attempt to enter the city until she knew
what was happening there.*

*I was frightened and I ran away from
my mother and she ran after me and
coaxed me to come back.*

'Look – if you have five pocket
calculators and I take two away, how
many have you got left?'

They took my name and address, took away all my possessions, and sent me down to the cells.

1 Match the sentences and phrases on the left with those on the right.

1 I had to get away.
2 I think of the new boy who ran away.
3 She has given away jewellery
4 The more you keep away from the shops,
5 These men wanted to help them keep their land,
6 I had accepted his offer because I wanted to break away –

A the less money you'll spend.
B worth millions of pounds.
C to break away from my family and community.
D not take it away from them.
E One way or another, I was going to leave Birmingham.
F Lane chased him and caught him.

1	2	3	4	5	6
E		B			

2 Choose the best alternative from the phrasal verbs
given to fill in the space provided.

1 Panic overcame Tim now and he turned and began to try to ....*run away*..........
across the rocks.
take away   run away   keep away

2 The best thing that you can do to avoid a cold is to ....*keep away*.......... from
anyone who has one.
give away   break away   keep away

3 Fontaine .... and founded the shortlived Nationalist Party.
    broke away   took away   gave away

4 I *took away* the knife *takes* from him. I don't know how.
    broke away   gave away   took away

5 'Could you *get away* early next week though?' 'Yes, that would be
    okay.'
    break away   get away   take away

3 **Write the correct form of the appropriate phrasal
    verb in the space provided.**

1 You should always ..... *keep* .... animals ...... *away* ..... from the kitchen.

2 France's plan to .... 30 million electronic telephone
    directories . . .

3 She let herself out and raced down the stairs and ...... *run away* .... along the
    road.

4 Another group ...... *break away* .... from the Labour Party the following year.

5 Let's go out for a walk to .... *get away* .... from it all.

6 She had ...... *take* .... the children .... with her
    to her parents' house.

BadJokes

4 **Find the logical ending for each of the jokes beginning
    on the left.**

1 Waiter, this soup isn't fit for a pig.   A You should have seen the one that got
2 What did the fisherman say when he   away!
    caught a bus?   B Take away the 't' and it becomes
3 How can you make a tea table into a   eatable.
    meal?   C Take away their credit cards.
4 How do you stop a herd of elephants   D The police made him bring it back.
    from charging?   E Sir, would you like me to take it away
5 What happened to the little boy who   and bring you some that is?
    ran away with the circus?

1	2	3	4	5
E	C	B	A	D

B Disappearing and Making things disappear

do away with   explain away   fade away   pass away   throw away

Our medicines have not <u>done away with</u>[1] disease.

All of this can, of course, <u>be explained away</u> for other reasons.

The sun's warmth began to <u>fade away</u>.

She <u>passed away</u>[2] within three weeks of her sister and mother.

30 million tonnes of refuse are <u>thrown away</u> in the UK.

◆ **LANGUAGE COMMENT**

1 **Eliminate** is a more formal word for **do away with**.

2 You use **pass away** when you want to avoid saying the word 'die'.

1 Write the correct phrasal verb to complete the following definitions.

1 If something ....*fades away*........., it slowly becomes less intense, frequent or common until it ends or disappears completely.

2 When you ......*throw away*.... something you no longer want or need, you get rid of it, for example by putting it in the dustbin.

3 If you ...*explain away*... a mistake or unpleasant situation, you give reasons to show that it is not as bad or important as people think.

4 To ......*eliminate*......... something means to get rid of it or abolish it.

2 Match the phrases on the left with those on the right.

1 He was seen on TV later,
2 Her new-found enthusiasm for running
3 Your husband sent the letter to us
4 She likes to keep things, even old things,
5 It would be nice to do away with

A all the paperwork that is usually involved.
B rather than throw them away.
C shortly before he passed away.
D explaining away his department's latest blunder.
E will soon fade away.

1	2	3	4	5
D	E	C	B	A

3 Choose the best alternative from the phrasal verbs
given to fill in the space provided.

1 Identity cards should be ..*done away with*.. , everybody has a passport
anyway.
explained away   done away with   faded away

2 'It was the last one my dad ever invented before he ...*passed away*........ .' 'His
final great work?' 'Exactly, Gordon.'
passed away   threw away   did away with

3 He did not ...*throw*... the pamphlet ...*away*.... , but he kept it in his desk.
fade away   throw away   explain away

4 It was vague rumour which would .....*fade away*...... and be forgotten.
pass away   explain away   fade away

5 Well, how do you ...*explain away*... the fact that we lost so much money last
year?
explain away   throw away   fade away

4 Write the correct form of the phrasal verb in the
space provided.

1 His guests were surprised when he ...*explained away*. the trick as 'a little
cheating'.

2 ...*Throw away*..... medicine after an illness. It's unlikely you'll use it again.

3 She's feeling very depressed at the moment: her mother ...*passed away*.
unexpectedly last month.

4 Let's ...*do away with*... the formalities and get down to business.

5 The music and laughter gradually ...*fade away*...... as the procession moved
off down the street.

Bad Jokes **5** Find the logical ending for each of
the jokes beginning on the left.

1 They don't throw the rubbish away.
2 Why did you throw your alarm clock
away?
3 I did my first television show a month
ago, and the next day five million sets
were sold.

A Because it always went off when I was
asleep.
B The people who couldn't sell theirs
threw them away.
C They make it into television shows.

1	2	3
B	A	C

5

C Other meanings

get away with hide away put away work away write away

I'm not going to allow Anne to get away with an offensive remark like that.

He looked at his drawings of the rocks and hid them away again.

Hamish began to put away a vast load of shopping he had brought home.

They haven't stopped, they've been working away[1] all day.

You just write away[2] giving your name, address and enclosing three tokens.

DONEGAN

'You again, Mr Philbean? Dear me, dear me, don't you ever get away with anything?'

◆ **LANGUAGE COMMENT**

1 **Beaver away, slave away, slog away,** and **toil away** mean almost the same as **work away.** These verbs are often used in a continuous tense.

2 **Send off** and **send away** mean almost the same as **write away.**

1 Write the correct phrasal verb to complete the following definitions.

1 If you ....*hide*.......... something ....*away*...... , you put it in a place where nobody else can find it.

2 If you ....*work away*............ , you continue working hard for a long time.

3 If you ....*put*............ something ....*away*..... , you place it tidily somewhere, for example in a cupboard, drawer, or pocket.

4 If you ....*write away*.... to a company or organization, you send them a letter asking for a product or information.

5 If you ....*get away with*.... something that you should not have done, you are not criticized or punished for doing it.

2 Match the sentences and phrases on the left with those
on the right.

1 You see, I may need somewhere
2 Why don't you write away
3 He had punched a teacher
4 What have you been doing with
   yourself?
5 We washed up in silence, Lally washing
   up,

A on the nose and got away with it.
B to hide away for a week or two.
C I've been working away at a book.
D the two of us drying and putting away.
E to them and ask for a catalogue?

1	2	3	4	5
B	D	A	C	D

3 Write the correct form of the appropriate phrasal
verb in the space provided.

1 I was able to keep warm as I .... in the snow.

2 He could make the most outrageous statements and somehow
   get away with...... it.

3 Albert folded the newspaper neatly and ....put........ it ...away...... on the side
   table.

4 I had to ...hide...... the presents ...away...... in the bedroom, so that the children
   wouldn't find them.

5 ...work away....... for it. It's cheaper by mail-order anyway.

4 Write a paragraph on the topic of your choice,
including at least one example of each of the phrasal
verbs you have just studied.

AWAY   **Revision exercises**

1 Choose the best alternative from the phrasal verbs
given to fill in the space provided.

1 You should .... those .... and get a pair of these.
   pass away   *throw away*   *run away*   *do away with*

2 In cross-examination Mr Stewart tried to .... the Police
   interest in Waddell.
   work away   *fade away*   *explain away*   *get away*

3 I've been .... on this project for the last two weeks.
   working away   *giving away*   *putting away*   *getting away with*

4 We cannot .... from the fact that a child is primarily an egoist.
   pass away   *break away*   *take away*   *get away*

5 You cannot .... violence by using violence.
   break away   *do away with*   *keep away*   *pass away*

6 Even a baby senses, I think, that she shouldn't be able to ....
   such tyranny. The habit is usually easy to break.
   run away   *hide away*   *do away with*   *get away with*

7 Australia, after it had .... from Antarctica, continued to drift
   northwards.
   run away   *faded away*   *broken away*   *put away*

8 You can .... £2,000 a year tax-free.
   explain away   *write away*   *give away*   *work away*

2 Now see if you can remember the meanings of AWAY
and the phrasal verbs you have been practising. Some
of the letters have been filled in to help you. You can
check your answers by looking at the list on page 1.

A W.*ith*. dr.*aw*.ing and
     S.e..p.ar....ating

b.*rea*.k away
g.et... away
g.ive.e away
k.ee...p away
r.un. away
t.ake.e away

B D.iss...ppoint.ing and
     M.o...ing th........s
     d...........

d.o. away w.ith.
e.x.plain.n away
f.ade. away
p.ass.s away
t.hrow. away

C Other meanings
g.et.... away w.ith.....
h.i..d.e. away
p.ut. away
w.ork.k away
wr.ite. away

BACK

Below are the two most important meanings of BACK. In all 12 phrasal verbs have been selected.

Under each of the headings you will see a list of the phrasal verbs which you are going to practise.

You can write other phrasal verbs with the same meaning in the space provided. Use a dictionary if necessary.

A Returning or Repeating something

bounce back
call back
fall back on
get back
give back
go back on
go back over
take back

....
....
....
....
....
....

B Controlling or Suppressing

cut back
fight back
hold back
set back

....
....
....
....
....

A Returning or Repeating something

**bounce back   call back   fall back on   get back
give back   go back on   go back over   take back**

*His life is one disaster after another, but he just
bounces back[1] every time.*

*Pitts called back[2] on Thursday, saying he hadn't been able
to make the arrangements.*

*We have a written script to fall back on if we run out of things
to discuss.*

*I left early yesterday and didn't get back till late. I had to
go up to London to see my lawyer.*

*Men do not consider their own needs enough and she wants
to give them back a pride in their appearance.*

*Penelope must have persuaded him that they could not
go back on their prior acceptance.*

Let's go back over[3] it one more time and see if we can find a solution.

We're going to take the typewriter back to the shop.

*'I'll be glad when this rest
break's over so we can get back
to some decent food'*

◆ **LANGUAGE COMMENT**

1 **Recover** is a more general word for **bounce back**.

2 **Phone back** and **ring back** are similar to **call back**, but **call back**
   can also mean to visit a place again.

3 **Go over** something **again** means almost the same as **go back over**.

1 Match the sentences and phrases on the left with those
on the right.

1 There was no point
2 They were totally useless,
3 After yesterday's fall,
4 It's a funny thing, the symptoms
   disappeared
5 If I didn't need the money,
6 The teacher could not go back on her
   word,
7 I'm sorry, Mr Smith is out.
8 He invariably falls back on

A and the guilty one would not own up.
B the Stock Market bounced back
   surprisingly quickly.
C He will call you back later.
D I would give it back again.
E but we wouldn't take them back to the
   shop.
F and he was soon feeling well enough to
   get back to work.
G in going back over it.
H sentimental clichés about peace and
   love.

1	2	3	4	5	6	7	8
C		D					

2 Choose the best alternative from the phrasal verbs
given to fill in the space provided.

1 Don't let us break up the party, but we have to .... before 11
   to take the baby-sitter home.
   give back call back get back

2 I .... the book .... to Indhar.
   bounced back gave back called back

3 When you see the hospital doctor, you may be asked to .... the
   same ground that you have covered.
   go back on go back over fall back on

4 Shops are often reluctant to .... unsatisfactory goods.
   take back give back get back

5 Mr Higson expects the market to .... quickly in April or May.
   bounce back give back go back on

6 So he did everything he could to persuade you to .... what
   you'd told us.
   call back go back on bounce back

7 I told him I would .... him .... when I had some news.
   bounce back call back go back over

3 Write the correct form of the appropriate phrasal
verb in the space provided.

1 Don't forget to .... your books .... to the library.

2 Don't you think we'd better .... to the subject you came to
   discuss?

3 I gave my word. I can't .... it.

4 I shall make some enquiries and .... you ....

5 I .... her .... her newspaper.

6 Teachers .... authority.

4 Write a paragraph on the topic of your choice,
including at least one example of each of the phrasal
verbs you have just studied.

B Controlling or Suppressing

cut back   fight back   hold back   set back

I did eliminate egg yolks and <u>cut back</u>[1] a bit on red meats. But I still enjoy eating out.

If we did that, the importing countries could <u>fight back</u>[2] with laws of their own.

The rise in living standards has been <u>held back</u> for so long.

This has <u>set back</u>[3] the whole programme of nuclear power in America.

'I've <u>cut back</u> on defence spending.'

◆ **LANGUAGE COMMENT**

1 **Reduce** is a more formal word for **cut back**. There is also a noun: *...the <u>cutback</u> in public services...*

2 **Retaliate** and **resist** are more formal words for **fight back**.

3 **Delay** is a more formal word for **set back**, and **hold up** means almost the same. There is also a noun: *The Union suffered a serious <u>setback</u>.*

1 Match the phrases on the left with those on the right.

1 When you cut back on dairy products,
2 Worry about the environment
3 The unusual cold of the early spring
4 We can't let them walk all over us,

A we have to find a way to fight back.
B had set them back with the painting.
C you cut back on cholesterol.
D has been one of the key restraints in holding back economic development.

1	2	3	4

2 Choose the best alternative from the phrasal verbs given to fill in the space provided.

1 Other countries have .... on high-priced Mexican oil.
cut back   set back   fought back

2 They need the money immediately and cannot .... their goods to push the price up.
set back   cut back   hold back

3 That computer failure has .... us .... at least a week.
fought back   cut back   set back

4 Our forces were .... desperately.
fighting back   holding back   setting back

3 Write the correct form of the appropriate phrasal
verb in the space provided.

1 Bad weather .... us .... by about three weeks.

2 If she is ambitious, don't try to .... her ....

3 The factory has .... its work force by 50%.

4 If someone hits you, you have to ....

4 Write a paragraph on the topic of your choice,
including at least one example of each of the phrasal
verbs you have just studied.

BACK **Revision exercises**

1 Choose the best alternative from the phrasal verbs
given to fill in the space provided.

1 Often you give up and .... easier solutions.
cut back   fall back on   sit back   set back

2 You can .... and collect your shoes tomorrow.
bounce back   get back   take back   call back

3 Benn stubbornly resisted all attempts to .... investment.
set back   take back   cut back   bounce back

4 He .... the schedule one more time just for my benefit.
went back over   set back   went back on   fell back on

5 Jamie's taken my jacket – make him .... it .... !
get back   give back   take back   go back on

6 Now you're .... what you told me earlier.
going back on   bouncing back   fighting back   setting back

7 There'll be a supper in the fridge for you if you .... from
Cambridge tonight.
give back   hold back   take back   get back

2 Match the two meanings of BACK with the pairs of
phrasal verbs given.

A Returning or Repeating something
B Controlling or Suppressing

1 go back on
   go back over ....

2 cut back
   fight back ....

3 get back
   give back ....

4 hold back
   set back ....

DOWN

Below are the four most important meanings of DOWN and one group of other meanings. In all 34 phrasal verbs have been selected.

Under each of the headings you will see a list of the phrasal verbs which you are going to practise. Some verbs appear more than once, as many phrasal verbs have more than one meaning.

You can write other phrasal verbs with the same meaning in the space provided. Use a dictionary if necessary.

A Decreasing and Reducing

bring down
calm down
come down
come down to
cut down
die down

keep down
narrow down
play down
run down
scale down
slow down

....
....
....

....
....
....
....
....
....
....

B Defeating and Suppressing

back down
bring down
clamp down
knock down
pull down
put down
wear down

....
....
....
....
....
....

D Writing and Recording

go down as
lay down
put down
put down to
take down

....
....
....
....

C Completing or Failing

break down
close down
let down
settle down
stand down
turn down

....
....
....
....
....
....

E Other meanings

get down to
live down
pin down
talk down to

....
....
....
....

A Decreasing and Reducing   Part 1

**bring down   calm down   come down   come down to
cut down   die down**

The promised measures included steps to <u>bring down</u> prices.

'Please, Mrs Kinter,' said Brody. '<u>Calm down</u>[1]. Let me explain.'

*Get on the phone at once, please, and offer to <u>come down</u> a couple of
hundred dollars.*

*Basically, it <u>comes down to</u> asking 'Is the workplace as safe for all
employees?'.*

Save time for yourself by <u>cutting your shopping down</u> to twice a week.

She waited until the laughter had <u>died down</u>[3] before going on.

*'I'd <u>cut down</u> on these
bourgeois sexist
occasions except people
might think I was
dieting.'*

◆ **LANGUAGE COMMENT**

1 **Settle down** means almost the same as **calm down**.

2 **Decrease** is a more formal word for **come down**; **go up** means the
opposite.

3 **Subside** is a more formal word for **die down**.

1 Write the correct phrasal verb to complete the
following definitions.

1 If a problem or question .... a particular thing, that is the most
important or relevant factor to be considered.

2 If something .... , it becomes much quieter or less intense.

3 If you .... something.................... , you reduce it or do it less often.

4 If the cost, level or amount of something .... , it becomes
cheaper or less than it was before.

2 Match the phrases on the left with those on the right.

1 The protests will soon die down,	A cannot cut down easily.
2 Modern technology contributes to bringing down	B but had no success.
3 There are dozens of contentious points,	C but in the end it comes down to planning.
4 Many smokers who are chemically addicted to nicotine	D you just have to wait.
5 An officer tried to calm them down	E has come down by 20% since 1975.
6 Local government expenditure	F the cost of fish in making available canned products.

1	2	3	4	5	6

3 Choose the best alternative from the phrasal verbs
given to fill in the space provided.

1 Ultimately, the problem .... the way in which housing has
been defined.
comes down to   cuts down   brings down

2 Although many businessmen realise they should .... on heavy
eating at lunch-time they often fool themselves.
calm down   cut down   bring down

3 He told me that things appeared to be .... a bit.
calming down   bringing down   cutting down

4 His anger takes a long time to ....
come down   come down to   die down

5 Swedish taxes have got to be ....
died down   brought down   calmed down

6 Birth rates in the Third World have started to .... more
rapidly.
come down   die down   cut down

4 Write the correct form of the appropriate phrasal
verb in the space provided.

1 Inflation is starting to ....

2 He has made a series of proposals which he believes would help
.... land prices.

3 When she had .... herself .... , she started the engine.

4 The wind has .... quite a lot.

5 The text was too long so we .... it ....

6 What it .... , I said, was that she had taken it as far as anyone
could be expected to do.

A Decreasing and Reducing   Part 2

keep down   narrow down   play down   run down   scale down   slow down

The French too are very concerned to try and keep costs down.

We finally narrowed down the list of candidates to three.

They have urged that the authorities should play down[1] the horrors of nuclear war.

Hospitals were being run down because of the spending cuts.

The project has been scaled down by about half of the original estimate.

Economic growth has slowed down[2] dramatically.

◆ **LANGUAGE COMMENT**

[1] **Exaggerate** and **play up** mean the opposite of **play down**.

[2] **Slow up** means almost the same as **slow down**; **speed up** means the opposite.

1 Write the correct phrasal verb to complete the following definitions.

1 If you .... something such as a choice or subject, you consider only the most suitable or important parts, and eliminate the rest.

2 If you .... something .... , you try to make people think that something is unimportant, or less important than it really is.

3 If an industry or organization is .... , its size, importance, or activity is deliberately reduced.

4 If you .... the number, size, or amount of something .... , you stop it increasing and try to keep it at a low level.

2 Match the phrases on the left with those on the right.

1 It's argued that our forces are so run down they	A the financial difficulties of the company.
2 We did not stop his southward advance	B don't deter anybody any more.
3 Keeping inflation down to an acceptable level	C is not as easy as it seems.
4 He will play down	D scaled down in importance.
5 How many suspects have we got?	E We've narrowed it down to four, sir.
6 Overall goals must be	F but did much to slow it down.

1	2	3	4	5	6

3 Choose the best alternative from the phrasal verbs given to fill in the space provided.

1 Malcolm needs to .... a little or he'll get an ulcer.
run down   slow down   narrow down

2 Public transport could be .... to the point where the car has achieved total dominance.
played down   narrowed down   run down

3 Let's .... the discussion .... , shall we?
narrow down   scale down   play down

4 Some aspects of reality are omitted or .... , while others are given more importance.
narrowed down   slowed down   played down

5 The project has been .... by about half the original estimate.
kept down   narrowed down   scaled down

6 Auction rooms are used to a plentiful flow of old documents, and this ....

prices ....
runs down   slows down   keeps down

4 Write the correct form of the phrasal verb in the space provided.

1 They .... the choice .... to about a dozen sites.

2 Their air forces had been ruinously ....

3 They've decided to .... the project because of a lack of government funding.

4 Harold .... the car ....

5 Can you .... the noise .... ?

6 We would like to stress that in no sense do we wish to .... the importance of the issues raised.

5 Write a paragraph on the topic of your choice, including at least one example of each of the phrasal verbs you have just studied.

B Defeating and Suppressing

**back down   bring down   clamp down   knock down
pull down   put down   wear down**

Eventually he <u>backed down</u> on the question of seating.

A national strike would <u>bring the government down</u>.

The authorities have got to <u>clamp down</u>[1] on these trouble makers.

I bumped into and nearly <u>knocked down</u> a person at the bus stop.

The council said it would close the flats and <u>pull them down</u>[2].

We've been encouraged all our life to <u>put down</u> women's talk.

It was one of the recognised nuisance-tactics designed to <u>wear down</u> the patience of the court.

◆ **LANGUAGE COMMENT**

1 **Crack down** means almost the same as **clamp down**.
Both exist as nouns:
...a <u>clampdown</u> on wasteful spending...
...a <u>crackdown</u> on criminals.

2 **Demolish** is a more formal word for **pull down**, and **knock down**
means almost the same; **put up** means the opposite of **pull down**.

1 Write the correct phrasal verb to complete the
following definitions.

1 To .... on people or activities means to take strong official
action to stop or control them.

2 If you .... people .... , you weaken them or their position by being
more persistent than they are.

3 If you .... on something, you accept someone else's point of
view or agree to do what they want you to do, even though you do not really want to.

2 Match the phrases on the left with those on the right.

1 Most commentators agree that this was
the issue which

2 The government issued orders

3 They tried to wear down the
management's resistance

4 She knew he wouldn't back down,

5 Don't drive so fast,

6 A lot of people will be delighted

7 The house was sold to James I in 1605

A you almost knocked that woman down.

B and was pulled down in the mid-
seventeenth century.

C by holding a series of strikes.

D brought down the SPD government in
May.

E to clamp down on the opposition.

F to see him put down.

G he had too much to lose.

1	2	3	4	5	6	7

3 Choose the best alternative from the phrasal verbs
given to fill in the space provided.

1 He fought with a kind of hideous, heedless, mechanical energy, slowly ....
   his man ....
   backing down   wearing down   clamping down

2 In the end I .... , it just wasn't worth losing a job over.
   backed down   knocked down   put down

3 Some of these street children are.. by cars as they dash
   among the traffic.
   put down   knocked down   backed down

4 Certain countries have .... on refugees seeking asylum.
   brought down   pulled down   clamped down

5 In the 1580s, Sir Francis Willoughby .... his family home at
   Wollaton and rebuilt it.
   brought down   pulled down   wore down

6 I don't intend to be .... so easily on questions of fact.
   backed down   clamped down   put down

7 In Poland unofficial strikes .... the unpopular Gomulka
   regime.
   brought down   knocked down   backed down

4 Write the correct form of the appropriate phrasal
verb in the space provided.

1 If someone .... you .... and is really mean and rotten to you, you
   should retaliate in some way.

2 Why did they .... all those houses .... ?

3 He threatened to prosecute us but he eventually ....

4 I was nearly .... by a hefty slap on the back.

5 These night calls are .... me ....

6 Lawrence Daly aggressively promised to .... the Government.

7 The Federal Reserve has .... on bank lending.

C Completing or Failing

**break down   close down   let down
settle down   stand down   turn down**

*An unhappy marriage which eventually breaks down[1]
often results in disturbed children.*

*If the firms failed to make enough money, they would
close down.*

*It would be best to run away now but she could not let
Jimmie down: he needed help.*

*Alan told her that after this, he would settle down and
marry her.*

*She was asked if she was prepared to stand down[2] in
favour of a younger candidate.*

*She applied for a job in a restaurant, but was turned
down[3].*

'Looks the kind of place a guy
could settle down, find a
woman, learn to read.'

◆ **LANGUAGE COMMENT**

1 **Break down** also exists as a noun:
There was a serious breakdown of communication.

2 **Step down** means almost the same as **stand down**.

3 **Reject** means almost the same as **turn down**.

1 Match the phrases on the left with those on the right.

1 I explained about his offer and said
2 At the end of July, the sewage system
   had broken down
3 If the President doesn't stand down
   before the election,
4 They felt strongly that
5 The mines had been closed down
6 You have to get a job

A the school system had let them down.
B following a geological survey.
C and the lavatories ceased to flush.
D and settle down.
E the next president will almost certainly
   be from the right.
F it was too good to turn down.

1	2	3	4	5	6

2 Choose the best alternative from the phrasal verbs
given to fill in the space provided.

1 No doubt about it, Jordache, you did well to .... the job in the
department.
settle down   close down   turn down

2 They're .... my old school.
closing down   standing down   breaking down

3 The talks .... over differences on doctrine.
broke down   turned down   let down

4 There were rumours that the Prime Minister would ....
break down   stand down   turn down

5 Charlie's never .... me .... yet.
broken down   let down   stood down

6 You're over forty now, you should .... and start thinking about
bringing up a family.
break down   settle down   let down

3 Write the correct form of the appropriate phrasal
verb in the space provided.

1 You're so silly. You regularly .... yourself .... , don't you?

2 I have .... an invitation for Saturday.

3 Garages are a handy institution whenever the car ....

4 Paul will never .... , he enjoys travelling too much.

5 The factory has had to be .... due to the recession.

6 She said, 'I'll .... if the meeting wants me to.'

4 Write a paragraph on the topic of your choice,
including at least one example of each of the phrasal
verbs you have just studied.

D Writing and Recording

**go down as   lay down   put down
put down to   take down**

*You, Freneau, would go down in history as
his assassin.*

*There are laws which lay down[1] what employers and
employees must and must not do.*

*You haven't put Professor Mangel's name down on
the list.*

All this can be put down to advances in engineering.

The postmistress began to take down[2] the message.

◆ LANGUAGE COMMENT

[1] **Stipulate** is a more formal word for **lay down**.

[2] **Copy down, jot down, note down** and **write down** all have similar
meanings.

1 Write the correct phrasal verb to complete the
following definitions.

1 When you .... words or numbers, you write or type them
somewhere.

2 If you .... what someone is saying, you listen to them and write
it down or record it.

3 If you .... one thing .... another thing, you believe that it is
caused by another thing.

4 If someone or something .... a particular thing, they are
regarded, remembered, or recorded as that thing.

5 If laws, rules, or people in authority .... what people should
do, they state that this is what must be done.

2 Match the phrases on the left with those on the right.

1 There were morning sessions for women and

2 He set up a tape recorder at Peter's bed

3 Sadly, they too grow up to be battering husbands. The phenomenon is put down

4 A government should lay down

5 Although this will go down as my day,

A he and Neil Foster were the real heroes.
B to take down anything he might say.
C my wife put down for Tuesdays and Thursdays.
D to the climate of violence in which the boy has grown up.
E national policy for various sectors of education.

1	2	3	4	5

3 Choose the best alternative from the phrasal verbs given to fill in the space provided.

1 I've never kept accounts. It's a mistake to .... what one spends, or to add up what comes in.
   go down as   put down   put down to

2 It seemed unsafe to .... anything .... coincidence.
   put down to   go down as   take down

3 He told her he would just like to .... her name and address.
   take down   put down to   go down as

4 These were the conditions .... by the Department of Health.
   taken down   laid down   put down to

5 This performance will .... one of the best ever seen.
   put down to   take down   go down as

4 Write the correct form of the appropriate phrasal verb in the space provided.

1 Jill was .... a story from Frank's dictation.

2 Planning is the key! Let the twenty-first century .... in history ....
   the century of planning!

3 The small thought .... in that 1968 report grew into a big idea.

4 The policy has been .... and agreed for years.

5 The whole thing will be .... the unfortunate fact that the crisis occurred while the boss was away.

E Other meanings

get down to live down pin down talk down to

*Sixth-form pupils look after the children while the mother
gets down to some serious teaching.*

If you were beaten by Jack, you'd never live it down.

*Police forces are continuing inquiries to try and
pin the whereabouts of the suspect down.*

*Parents can't dictate to their adolescent children or
talk down to them.*

*'If I have to pin it down to one thing I
would say your most attractive
feature is your wallet!'*

1 Write the correct phrasal verb to
complete the following definitions.

1 If someone .... you, they talk to you in a way that shows that
they think they are more important or more clever than you.

2 If you are unable to .... a mistake, failure, or foolish action,
you are unable to make people forget that you did it.

3 If you try to .... something which is hard to define or describe,
you try to say exactly what it is or what it is like.

4 When you .... something, you start doing it seriously and with
a lot of attention.

2 Match the phrases on the left with those on the right.

1 The more he tried to pin them down   A you won't live this down.
2 Children always sense immediately   B we were able to get down to the
3 When some of the terrible tension   business of the session.
    subsided,   C when you are talking down to them.
4 Even if you live to be a hundred,   D on what they were talking about the
                                           vaguer they got.

1	2	3	4

3 Write the correct form of the appropriate phrasal verb.

1 I think it would be best if we .... business.

2 It is the story of a girl who finds it impossible to .... her past.

3 He .... everybody – he likes to think he's better than we are.

4 He was anxious to .... the Minister .... to a decision.

DOWN Revision exercises

1 **Choose the best alternative from the phrasal verbs given to fill in the space provided.**

1 In Britain, by contrast, self-made men often try to .... their social origins.
bring down   play down   narrow down   stand down

2 The real choice is whether I can afford to .... the money Bob is offering.
turn down   wear down   take down   put down

3 Saunders then .... the business in hand.
went down as   put down to   got down to   let down

4 A bus came screeching to a stop, practically .... him ....
slowing down   standing down   putting down   knocking down

5 If he .... us .... again, we'll have to find someone else to do the work.
lives down   lets down   breaks down   dies down

6 The fight to .... inflation and reduce unemployment must be our first priority.
come down   turn down   lay down   bring down

7 The police have to .... on drug smuggling.
clamp down   scale down   pin down   close down

8 If you can also spell and .... a telephone message correctly you will be a real asset to the firm.
put down   pull down   take down   run down

9 The fighting .... overnight.
turned down   died down   closed down   pinned down

10 Whatever happens tomorrow, she'll .... in history .... a great stateswoman.
go down as   put down to   come down to   talk down to

11 He said he would .... at the end of the year.
keep down   live down   bring down   stand down

12 Try to .... him .... to a date.
put down   take down   pin down   cut down

13 Making this project confidential is partly so that it can be more effective and partly to
.... the number of people who know what is going on.
keep down   clamp down   let down   talk down to

14 The most obvious piece of advice, therefore, is to .... in any way possible. (Preferably to zero!)
    calm down   bring down   wear down   cut down

15 It's only gradually that the barriers between the sexes are ....
    settled down   broken down   calmed down   lived down

16 She has an infuriating habit of .... people .... in small ways.
    narrowing down   putting down   closing down   standing down

2 Complete the phrasal verbs in groups A–D below. When you have finished, check your answers on page 15.

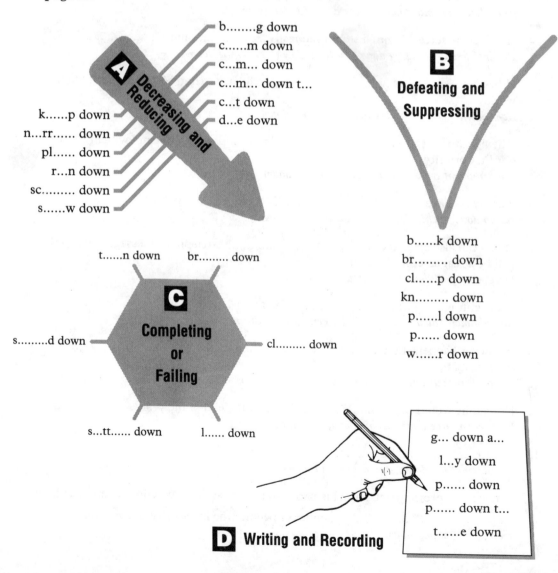

A Decreasing and Reducing

b........g down
c.....m down
c...m... down
c...m... down t...
c...t down
d...e down

k......p down
n...rr...... down
pl...... down
r...n down
sc......... down
s......w down

B Defeating and Suppressing

b......k down
br......... down
cl......p down
kn......... down
p......l down
p...... down
w......r down

C Completing or Failing

t......n down   br......... down

s.........d down   cl......... down

s...tt...... down   l...... down

D Writing and Recording

g... down a...
l...y down
p...... down
p...... down t...
t......e down

IN

Below are the four most important meanings of IN and one group of other meanings. In all 24 phrasal verbs have been selected.

Under each of the headings you will see a list of the phrasal verbs you are going to practise. Some verbs appear more than once, as many phrasal verbs have more than one meaning.

You can write other phrasal verbs with the same meaning in the space provided. Use a dictionary if necessary.

A Inserting and Absorbing

plug in
put in
sink in
take in

....
....
....
....
....

B Including

fit in
fit in with
take in
throw in

....
....
....
....
....

C Being involved and active

call in
come in
fill in
go in for
join in
put in
settle in

....
....
....
....
....
....
....
....

D Beginning

bring in
come in
phase in
set in

....
....
....

E Other meanings

come in for
fill in (two meanings)
give in
stay in

....
....
....
....
....
....

A   Inserting and Absorbing

plug in   put in   sink in   take in

*A television set is a fire risk if left <u>plugged in</u>[1]
over night.*

*If you pour hot water into a glass, <u>put a spoon in</u>[2]
first to absorb the heat.*

It took a moment or two for her words to <u>sink in</u>.

*Mrs Stannard shook hands, her eyes <u>taking in</u>
Karin from head to foot.*

'Perhaps we have to <u>plug it in</u> ourselves.'

◆ **LANGUAGE COMMENT**

1 **Unplug** means the opposite of **plug in**.

2 **Stick in** means almost the same as **put in**.

1 **Match the phrases on the left with those on the right.**

1 He puts in the coins
2 The prisoners had nothing to do
3 Alex had been the perfect pupil,
4 He put on a record

A listening and watching and taking it in.
B and plugged in the earphones.
C and dials the number in Toulouse.
D but let their situation sink in.

1	2	3	4

2 **Choose the best alternative from the phrasal verbs
given to fill in the space provided.**

1 All machines work better if you .... them ....
   take in   sink in   plug in

2 I smelt it, and at first it smelt like chlorine which is ....
   swimming pools.
   taken in   put in   sunk in

3 The implications of this did not at first ....
   sink in   put in   plug in

4 I didn't .... all he was saying.
   take in   sink in   plug in

3 Write the correct form of the phrasal verb in the space provided.

1 The lady across the aisle showed him how to .... his headphones

....

2 As he read out the documents and explained them, I .... few of these details.

3 To design a car that goes faster the designer could either .... a more powerful engine, or reduce the weight.

4 Has any of what I've been saying .... ?

4 Write a paragraph on the topic of your choice, including at least one example of each of the phrasal verbs you have just studied.

B Including

fit in fit in with take in throw in

You seem to fit in[1] an enormous amount of work every day.

They manufacture mild steel to fit in with[2] modern methods of production.

I flew on to California, deciding to take in Florida on the way home.

We only had to pay £9 for bed and breakfast, with lunch thrown in.

◆ **LANGUAGE COMMENT**

1 **Squeeze in** and **work in** mean almost the same as **fit in**.

2 **Tie in with** means almost the same as **fit in with**.

1 **Write the correct phrasal verb to complete the following definitions.**

1 If you .... something such as a film, a museum, or a place, while you are on holiday or travelling somewhere, you go to see it or visit it.

2 If you .... an extra item when you are selling some thing or arranging something, you add it or include it in order to persuade people to buy the thing or accept the arrangement.

3 If you manage to .... a person or task, you manage to find time to deal with them.

4 If something .... a system, method, idea, or situation, it is suitable and works successfully as part of it.

2 **Match the phrases on the left with those on the right.**

1 The old sort of love no longer
2 Americans go up to Oxford and
3 A few minor reforms had been
4 I'm on holiday next week,

A but I can fit you in on the 9th.
B fits in with our changing needs.
C thrown in to sweeten the temper of the local people.
D take in the Cotswolds in a day.

1	2	3	4

3 Choose the best alternative from the phrasal verbs
given to fill in the space provided.

1 He .... the software for the same price.
took in fitted in threw in

2 The guided tour .... most of the famous architectural sites of
Turkey.
took in fitted in with threw in

3 I'll try to .... a visit to the school while I'm in Edinburgh, but
I'm not promising anything.
throw in fit in fit in with

4 I'm willing to .... your way of doing things.
throw in fit in with fit in

4 Write the correct form of the appropriate phrasal
verb in the space provided.

1 They can't do it today, so they will .... it .... when they have a
van in that area.

2 They .... the matching handbag for another hundred francs.

3 I don't think that'll .... very well .... the present system.

4 As a woman's world widens from a small domestic centre to
.... the complexities of the outside world . . .

5 Write a paragraph on the topic of your choice,
including at least one example of each of the phrasal
verbs you have just studied.

33

C Being involved and active

call in   come in   fill in   go in for   join in   put in   settle in

Riot squads known to every Frenchman simply as the CRS were called in[1] and for the first time armed with submachine guns.

Let me just come in[2] on this, because Clive is not giving the whole story.

I'll fill you in on the details now.

I don't go in for that sort of fishing.

When other games are played, he tries to join in.

Half of them were putting in forty-five hours a week or more.

Madame Maire gave her three weeks to settle in.

◆ **LANGUAGE COMMENT**

1 **Bring in** means almost the same as **call in**.

2 **Barge in, break in, butt in** and **cut in** are all similar in meaning, but they often suggest a rude interruption, whereas **come in** does not.

1 **Match the sentences and phrases on the left with those on the right.**

1 Eric, would you like to come in here
2 Then they began to sing
3 How's the new teacher settling in?
4 Come back to the office and
5 I was certainly pleased by
6 Before you call in the water board,
7 Her father was a builder and decorator in Birmingham,

A I'll fill you in.
B check that the pipes are not frozen.
C and she went in for drama without really knowing what it was.
D to give us your views on the matter.
E and in a moment all the voices joined in.
F He's still a little lost, actually.
G the level of effort everyone put in today.

1	2	3	4	5	6	7

2 Choose the best alternative from the phrasal verbs
given to fill in the space provided.

1 I've never .... jewellery.
   gone in for come in put in

2 Is this a private fight or can anyone .... ?
   call in fill in join in

3 Had he but asked, he could undoubtedly have .... men of the
   highest international eminence.
   joined in called in settled in

4 He needs to be .... on the situation in Vietnam.
   put in filled in come in

5 There's plenty of time to get ....
   settled in put in called in

6 Could I .... here? I do happen to have quite a lot of experience
   in this field.
   call in go in for come in

7 During the campaign, the President has been .... 80 hour
   weeks that seem to include endless White House dinners.
   filling in putting in coming in

3 Write the correct form of the appropriate phrasal
verb in the space provided.

1 Kate should be able to .... you .... on what's been happening
   since you've been away.

2 We .... the police and accused the boys of stealing.

3 He had worked hard all his life, ... overtime at the plant
   whenever he could get it.

4 They raced round the Lakes on high-powered motor-bikes, and
   .... prodigious drinking sessions.

5 Jane, would you like to .... here?

6 And how are you .... , Mr Swallow?

7 Several people .... the applause.

D Beginning

bring in come in phase in set in

We intend to <u>bring in</u> legislation to control their activities.

Years ago, when miniskirts first <u>came in</u>, all the girls rushed to buy them.

Beveridge's original plan was to <u>phase in</u>[1] adequate old-age pensions in the period up to 1956.

By the time he had got it back in place, panic had <u>set in</u>[2].

◆ LANGUAGE COMMENT

[1] **Phase out** means the opposite of **phase in**.

[2] This meaning of **set in** is only used of something unpleasant.

1 Match the phrases on the left with those on the right.

1 There is probably more than enough time	A brought in a new Trade Disputes Act.
2 They had to find a roof to live under	B to phase in this enormous resource well before fossil fuels become exhausted.
3 The Labour Government in 1965	C before natural gas came in.
4 We used coal gas	D before the cold weather set in.

1	2	3	4

2 Choose the best alternative from the phrasal verbs given to fill in the space provided.

1 We're .... the new computer system .... over a period of three years.
coming in   setting in   phasing in

2 Every year the fashion changes: new colours .... and styles change.
bring in   come in   set in

3 The bad weather has .... for the winter.
set in   phased in   brought in

4 The Lloyd George Government .... the Munitions Act of 1915.
set in   came in   brought in

3 Write the correct form of the appropriate phrasal
verb in the space provided.

1 The Health and Safety at Work Act .... last year.

2 A quarter of a million workers won local agreements to .... a
thirty-nine-hour week much sooner.

3 Technology offers many alternatives that could be ....

4 A feeling of anti-climax ....

4 Write a paragraph on the topic of your choice,
including at least one example of each of the phrasal
verbs you have just studied.

E Other meanings

come in for fill in give in stay in

British industry does <u>come in for</u> a great deal of criticism.

We <u>filled in</u>[1] all the customs forms.

One of the other girls is sick and I said I'd <u>fill in</u>[2].

You certainly don't <u>give in</u>[3] and meekly let the child have her way.

We <u>stayed in</u>[4] the whole evening, didn't go to the disco at all.

'I know what – let's <u>stay in</u> and get some fresh air.'

◆ **LANGUAGE COMMENT**

1 **Fill out** means almost the same as **fill in**.

2 **Stand in** means almost the same as **fill in**.

3 **Surrender** and **back down** mean almost the same as **give in**.

4 **Stop in** means almost the same as **stay in**.

1 Write the correct phrasal verb to complete the following definitions.

1 If you .... , you admit that you will have to do something you have been trying not to do, or that you will not be able to do something you wanted to do.

2 If you .... , you remain at home rather than going out and enjoying yourself.

3 If you .... for someone, you do the work that they normally do because they are temporarily unable to do it.

4 If you .... a form, you write all the information that is requested in the appropriate spaces.

5 If someone or something .... criticism, blame, or abuse, they are criticized, blamed, or insulted.

2 Match the sentences and phrases on the left with those
on the right.

1 Ask for a claim form, fill it in
2 She was a domineering woman
3 The October index of basic wage rates
   due on Thursday
4 I've got to go to the doctor's this
   afternoon.
5 I can't go out tonight,

A and send it to the social security
   office.
B Can you fill in for me?
C I have to stay in and work.
D and she didn't normally give in so
   easily.
E will come in for special scrutiny.

1	2	3	4	5

3 Write the correct form of the appropriate phrasal
verb in the space provided.

1 I don't like going out much, I prefer .... with a good book.

2 Who's .... for Gordon next week?

3 .... your name and address here.

4 She was certain only of one thing – she would not .... to them.

5 His son, who had sponsored their publication, ... for some
adverse criticism.

4 Write a paragraph on the topic of your choice,
including at least one example of each of the phrasal
verbs you have just studied.

IN Revision exercise

1 Choose the best alternative from the phrasal verbs
given to fill in the space provided.

1 I'm very busy at the moment, but I'll try and .... you .... on
Friday afternoon.
call in   join in   phase in   fit in

2 Does this .... what you were doing on 'Quality'?
fit in   fit in with   come in for   set in

3 If you .... the furniture .... , it's a deal.
throw in   come in   give in   go in for

4 Sorry, I'd just like to .... here to clarify a few points.
bring in   come in   put in   settle in

5 The first volume took me a couple of years during which I seldom
.... less than fifteen hours of work daily.
took in   put in   stayed in   threw in

6 We're .... nicely, thank you.
setting in   fitting in with   settling in   filling in

7 I think we should .... it .... , rather than get rid of the old system
altogether.
bring in   phase in   join in   plug in

8 I'm sorry I missed the meeting. Could you .... me .... on what
happened?
fill in   bring in   call in   sink in

9 It must be treated quickly before infection ....
settles in   joins in   sets in   takes in

10 Acts covering agriculture were .... in 1952 and 1956.
come in   sunk in   called in   brought in

11 She .... to the temptation of lying around in bed all day.
gave in   took in   joined in   put in

12 I hope you're .... all this .... – the exam's on Monday remember.
sinking in   taking in   settling in   staying in

13 We need some extra help, we can't keep .... for people when
they're sick.
fitting in   putting in   joining in   filling in

14 .... something gentle and uncompetitive like yoga.
Come in for   Give in   Go in for   Fit in with

OFF

Below are the five most important meanings of OFF and one group of other meanings. In all 29 phrasal verbs have been selected.

Under each of the headings you will see a list of the phrasal verbs which you are going to practise. Some verbs appear more than once, as many phrasal verbs have more than one meaning.

You can write other phrasal verbs with the same meaning in the space provided. Use a dictionary if necessary.

A Leaving and Beginning

drop off
kick off
see off
set off
spark off
take off

....

....

....

....

....

....

....

B Rejecting and Preventing

hold off
keep off
lay off
put off
write off

....

....

....

....

....

C Stopping and Cancelling

break off
call off
let off
take off

....

....

....

....

D Decreasing

cool off
fall off
level off
wear off
work off

....

....

....

....

E Finishing and Completing

finish off
go off
pay off
pull off

....

....

....

....

F Other meanings

go off (two meanings)
rip off
show off
tell off

....

....

....

....

A Leaving and Beginning

drop off kick off see off set off spark off take off

I can *drop Daisy off* on my way home.

They *kicked off* a two-month tour of the U.S. with a party in Washington.

She *saw him off* at the station.

He *set off*[1] on another of his European pleasure tours.

There was a risk that the decision would *spark off*[2] a conflict.

A steady stream of aircraft was *taking off* and landing.

◆ **LANGUAGE COMMENT**

1 **Set out, start out** and **start off** mean almost the same as **set off**.

2 **Trigger off** and **set off** mean almost the same as **spark off**.

1 Write the correct phrasal verb to complete the following definitions.

1 If one thing ...*sparks off*... a state or event, it causes the state or event to exist or happen, often by accident.

2 When you ...*see*... someone ...*off*..., you go with them to the station, airport, or port that they are leaving from, and say goodbye to them there.

3 When you ...*trigger off*... an event or discussion, you start it.

4 When you ...*set off*..., you start a journey.

2 Match the sentences and phrases on the left with those on the right.

1 If no one is seeing you off,
2 Could you drop me off at the post office?
3 Are we ready for the debate?
4 His letter of praise and support at that time
5 The strike caused the collapse of many small businesses
6 We set off

A Right. Who kicks off?
B which might, eventually, have taken off.
C on another four-hour trek through the swamps.
D I'll take you.
E I have to send a parcel.
F had sparked off a friendship between the two men.

1	2	3	4	5	6
D	E	A	F	B	C

42

3 **Choose the best alternative from the phrasal verbs given to fill in the space provided.**

1 His comment ....*sparked off*.......... a debate on the economic policies of the present government.
sparked off took off dropped off

2 Okay. Let's ....*kick off*.......... by discussing the new software.
set off kick off drop off

3 Are you ......*seeing*...... someone ......*off*...... too?
setting off seeing off kicking off

4 Why are you so late? Oh, I had to ......*drop*...... my wife ......*off*...... , her car's at the garage.
take off set off drop off

5 Dan ....*set off*.......... down the mountain to find help.
dropped off sparked off set off

6 Money-market funds have ....*taken off*.......... faster than the space shuttle.
dropped off sparked off taken off

4 **Write the correct form of the appropriate phrasal verb in the space provided.**

1 Do-it-yourself began seriously to ......*take*......*off*...... in the 1930s.

2 Also there to ......*see*...... us ......*off*...... was John Ryan.

3 Every morning I have to ......*drop*.... the kids ......*off*...... at school.

4 We're ....*set off*.......... early on Sunday morning to avoid the traffic.

5 Can they meet the demand ....*triggered*......*off* by the boom in TV video?

6 At 10 p.m. Prince Charles ....*set*......*off*...... 45 minutes of fireworks.

5 **Write a paragraph on the topic of your choice, including at least one example of each of the phrasal verbs you have just studied.**

B Rejecting and Preventing

hold off   keep off   lay off   put off   write off

The French and British wanted to <u>hold off</u> Portuguese textile competition as long as possible.

If you don't <u>keep off</u> the street with your bicycle, I'll take it away.

So if demand falls, the company <u>lays men off</u>[1].

Don't <u>put it off</u> till tomorrow.

'Whatever you do,' she pleaded, 'don't <u>write off</u> philosophy without even trying it'.

'Put it off? Because of a little shower?'

◆ **LANGUAGE COMMENT**

1 There is also a noun:
   Textile companies announced 2,000 fresh <u>layoffs</u> last week.

1 Write the correct phrasal verb to complete the following definitions.

1 If you .... someone or something .... , you decide that they are unimportant, useless, or unlikely to be successful and that they are not worth further consideration.

2 If you .... an event or appointment, you delay or postpone it.

3 If you .... an enemy, an opponent, or an attack, you prevent them from successfully attacking you or competing against you.

4 If workers are .... , they are told by their employer that they have to leave their jobs because there is no more work for them to do.

2 Match the sentences and phrases on the left with those on the right.

1 He can't be put off any more.
2 Laying off workers
3 What did your father say about your writing off his car?
4 She had a veil pulled down all round her hat
5 Everyone holds off buying as long as they can,

A if they think the price is going to come down.
B is not necessarily a solution to our financial problems.
C to keep off the flies.
D Leaving out the swear words - nothing!
E You'll have to see him this week.

1	2	3	4	5

3 Choose the best alternative from the phrasal verbs
given to fill in the space provided.

1 They did not have enough ammunition left to .... another
charge if the enemy came in strong and hard.
lay off   hold off   write off

2 The directors made plans to .... 3,000 workers.
lay off   keep off   put off

3 I .... starting it time and again, frightened of the sheer scale of
the project.
write off   keep off   put off

4 You can't .... them .... just because we haven't heard from them
for four days. Give them a bit longer.
hold off   keep off   write off

5 There is going to be a revolution, so .... the roads.
hold off   keep off   put off

4 Write the correct form of the appropriate phrasal
verb in the space provided.

1 They kept .... signing the paper.

2 Having a job helps .... them .... the streets.

3 They were able to .... a very much superior attacking force.

4 City workers are being .... at the rate of 100 a week.

5 Should an insured car be .... in an accident, the insurers will
usually pay the current value of the vehicle.

5 Write a paragraph on the topic of your choice,
including at least one example of each of the phrasal
verbs you have just studied.

C Stopping and Cancelling

break off call off let off take off

Diplomatic relations were restored after being broken off during the war.

On the eve of her departure the strike was definitely called off, and she was sure of her flight.

We have been let off our homework because of the concert.

Bill and I took time off from work and flew to France.

'Well, thank goodness common sense has prevailed. It seems Gascoigne's agent has let the referee off with a severe warning.'

1 **Match the phrases on the left with those on the right.**

1 If you can't behave yourself,
2 Until further notice I have been taken off
3 He believes that if he works all day
4 Men seem to be more skilled at

A he should be let off domestic chores.
B breaking off relationships than women.
C we might as well call the whole thing off.
D all routine duties and given a rather special job.

1	2	3	4

2 **Choose the best alternative from the phrasal verbs given to fill in the space provided.**

1 She arranged with the principal of her school to .... the necessary time from school.
   break off let off take off

2 Then things began to go wrong. He .... the relationship.
   broke off let off took off

3 The boss .... us .... work early because of the public holiday tomorrow.
   broke off called off let off

4 Classes will be .... on Thursday and Friday.
   taken off called off broken off

3 Write the correct form of the appropriate phrasal
verb in the space provided.

1 They hoped that the strike would be ....

2 With that, Cities Service .... the merger talks.

3 You have to .... Christmas Day as a holiday.

4 He .... me .... with a reprimand.

4 Write a paragraph on the topic of your choice,
including at least one example of each of the phrasal
verbs you have just studied.

D Decreasing

cool off fall off level off wear off work off

We cooled off from the heat with a refreshing swim.

We knew that the numbers of overseas students would fall off[1] drastically.

This growth in demand levelled off[2] after 1973.

The effect of the aspirin had worn off and her toothache had come back.

We should all be able to work off our stress physically.

'Of course, I've had to diversify a bit since the crowds fell off.'

◆ **LANGUAGE COMMENT**

1 **Drop** means almost the same as **fall off**, and **ease off** and **slacken off** have similar meanings.

2 **Stabilize** is a more formal word for **level off**. **Level out** means the same as **level off**.

1 **Match the phrases on the left with those on the right.**

1 By the next afternoon
2 He had given us as much food as we could eat,
3 The population will probably reach 320 million
4 As the weather cooled off
5 The flow of western capital is falling off

A he exchanged the robe for a thick blanket.
B just when it is most needed.
C before levelling off.
D the shock had worn off.
E and wouldn't hear of letting us work off our meal.

1	2	3	4	5

2 Choose the best alternative from the phrasal verbs
given to fill in the space provided.

1 When it starts to .... , take another tablet.
work off   level off   wear off

2 The curve of natural economic growth was almost certainly starting to

....
level off   cool off   work off

3 I need to .... some of this extra weight I'm carrying around.
level off   work off   wear off

4 Vita's love for him was ....
falling off   cooling off   working off

5 Economic growth in the Far East will .... only slightly.
fall off   cool off   work off

3 Write the correct form of the appropriate phrasal
verb in the space provided.

1 He used to .... his anger by listening to very loud and very
heavy music.

2 They forecast that cheque volumes will soon stagnate at around 3.7 billion and begin

to .... at the end of the decade.

3 He seems to have .... on the negotiation idea.

4 Property values are continuing to go down, but estate agents say that they may soon

....

5 The pain soon ....

4 Write a paragraph on the topic of your choice,
including at least one example of each of the phrasal
verbs you have just studied.

E Finishing and Completing

finish off go off pay off pull off

We had to work until midnight to finish them off[1].

The ceremony at the Arc de Triomphe went off[2] exactly as planned.

He had used the firm's money to pay off[3] gambling debts.

You have just pulled off[4] one of the biggest arms deals in the twentieth century.

24 HOURS TO PAYOFF GAMBLING DEBTS. PLEASE GIVE GENEROUSLY

◆ **LANGUAGE COMMENT**

1 **Polish off** is an informal expression for **finish off**.
2 **Pass off** means almost the same as **go off**.
3 **Repay** means almost the same as **pay off**.
4 **Bring off** and **carry off** mean almost the same as **pull off**.

1 **Match the phrases on the left with those on the right.**

1 The most common reason for borrowing
2 He had cooked a chicken
3 To Francois's great joy the introduction went off
4 She had succeeded, triumphantly:

A without a flaw.
B she had pulled it off.
C and the two of them finished it off together at one sitting.
D is to pay off existing loans.

1	2	3	4

2 **Choose the best alternative from the phrasal verbs given to fill in the space provided.**

1 I've had problems .... the job.
   finishing off paying off going off

2 Before leaving Cape Town I tried to .... a minor academic miracle.
   pull off pay off go off

3   The last formalities .... without a hitch.
    pulled off   went off   finished off

4   How long will it take to .... the loan ....? Ten years? Twenty?
    pull off   pay off   go off

3 Write the correct form of the appropriate phrasal
    verb in the space provided.

1   We decided to go back and .... the wine.

2   One could not .... such a surrealistic venture without investing
    an enormous amount of time and money.

3   The show .... magnificently, especially the special effects.

4   So she fell into debt and had to .... it .... by selling her house.

4 Write a paragraph on the topic of your choice,
    including at least one example of each of the phrasal
    verbs you have just studied.

F Other meanings

go off rip off show off tell off

The gun went off as he was putting it away.

Food that has 'gone off¹' has been infected with bacteria that cause illness.

The local shopkeepers were all trying to rip off² the tourists.

He was afraid the others might think he was showing off³ or being superior.

When I was told off⁴ by my parents, it was nearly always justified.

'Take no notice – he's *showing off*.'

◆ **LANGUAGE COMMENT**

1 **Decay** is a more formal word for **go off**.

2 **Rip off** is very informal. **Cheat** means almost the same as **rip off**.
   There is also a noun:
   They knew it was a rip-off.

3 This meaning of **show off** is used to show disapproval.

4 **Reprimand** is a formal word for **tell off**.

1 Write the correct phrasal verb to complete the
following definitions.

1 If someone .... you .... , they cheat you by charging you too much
money for something.

2 If you .... , you try to impress people by making your skills or
good qualities very obvious.

3 If food or drink .... , it becomes stale, sour, or rotten.

4 If a gun .... , it is fired; if a bomb .... ,
it explodes.

5 If you .... someone .... , you speak to them angrily because they
have done something wrong.

2 Match the sentences and phrases on the left with those on the right.

1 Stop showing off.
2 The court wastes my time
3 Smell this, will you?
4 Don't tell me off again, dad,
5 The probability of a nuclear weapon

A going off by accident is slight.
B Can't you see everybody's bored with your war stories.
C and the lawyers rip me off!
D I think it's gone off.
E I did my best.

1	2	3	4	5

3 Write the correct form of the appropriate phrasal verb in the space provided.

1 The milk's .... again.

2 I'm fed up of people thinking they can .... me .... just because I'm a foreigner.

3 My mother .... me .... for not clearing up my room.

4 I could hear the bombs ....

5 There were lots of kids .... on the diving board.

OFF Revision exercise

1 Choose the best alternative from the phrasal verbs given to fill in the space provided.

1 Bradlee was one of the few persons who could *write off* that kind of thing
....
drop off   pull off   write off   tell off

2 This incident could ....*spark off*.... another war.
rip off   let off   spark off   pull off

3 It was the new delegates who tried to ...*call off*.......... Thursday's march before it was too late.
fall off   pay off   drop off   call off

4 Do not sound harrassed, or you will be ...*written off*..... as a hysterical woman.
written off   held off   put off   kicked off

5 Remember food ..*goes off*.......... very quickly in this heat.
kicks off   holds off   finishes off   goes off

6 There are rumours that British Leyland are going to ...*lay off ?*.......... another 1,000 workers.
wear off   lay off   work off   set off

7 At exactly four minutes to three they ...*set off*............ .
set off   sparked off   ripped off   called off

8 The effect of the drug won't ...*wear off*.......... until tonight.
break off   let off   wear off   put off

9 He was eager to ...*show off*..... the new car.
cut off   tell off   fall off   show off

10 At best they lose some money by being ...*laid off*........... work for a while.
told off   laid off   finished off   paid off

11 As it happened the meeting ...*went off*........ well.
pulled off   put off   went off   showed off

12 These metal attachments normally take longer than that to ...*cool off*........ .
go off   spark off   set off   cool off

13 The pilot turned the plane into the wind to ...*take off*.......... .
hold off   take off   work off   rip off

14 The Apache warriors ...*cut off*.......... the fight and carried his bleeding body away.
broke off   cut off   saw off   wore off

15 The boss has ...*told off*...her *written off*... for taking long lunch breaks.
worn off   worked off   told off   written off

ON

Below are the three most important meanings of ON and one group of other meanings. In all 21 phrasal verbs have been selected.

Under each of the headings you will see a list of the phrasal verbs you are going to practise. Some verbs appear more than once, as many phrasal verbs have more than one meaning.

You can write other phrasal verbs with the same meaning in the space provided. Use a dictionary if necessary.

A Continuing

drag on
get on
go on
keep on
pass on
ramble on
stay on

....

....

....

....

....

....

B Progressing

come on
get on
move on
urge on

....

....

....

....

....

C Beginning

bring on
catch on
come on
move on to

....

....

....

....

D Other meanings

get on
go on (two meanings)
lay on
look on
take on

....

....

....

....

....

....

A Continuing

**drag on   get on   go on   keep on
pass on   ramble on   stay on**

*Some legal cases have <u>dragged on</u>[1] for eight
years.*

Perhaps we can <u>get on</u> with the meeting.

*She turned to Poirot again. 'Yes, <u>go on</u>.[2]
<u>Go on</u> finding out.*

*Only half the workforce will be <u>kept on</u>
after this order has been completed.*

*The union head office may be able to <u>pass
on</u>[3] helpful information, or it could put you
in touch with someone who will be able to
help you.*

*The professor was always <u>rambling on</u>
about his favourite subject.*

Pupils have to <u>stay on</u>[4] at school till they are 16.

*'Would the gifted children <u>carry on</u> quietly
with the chapter on Propositional Calculus.'*

◆ **LANGUAGE COMMENT**

1 **Drag along** means the same as **drag on**.

2 **Carry on** and **keep on** mean almost the same as **go on**. All of them
   are followed by an '-ing' form (gerund).

3 **Send on** is similar to **pass on** except it implies sending something by
   post.

4 **Leave** means the opposite of **stay on**.

1 Write the correct phrasal verb to complete the
following definitions.

1 If you .... doing something, you continue to do it.

2 If someone.. , they talk or write for a long time in a rather
confused and disordered way.

3 If an event or process .... , it progresses very slowly and takes
longer than seems necessary.

4 If you .... with an activity, you start doing or continue
doing it.

5 If you .... someone .... at work or school, you continue to employ
them or continue to educate them.

2 Match the sentences and phrases on the left with those on the right.

1 She had to start work while her brothers
2 The weeks dragged on,
3 I love playing golf – I could go on playing like this forever.
4 What is he rambling on about?
5 I always pass on good advice.
6 However, I'm seriously thinking of letting her stay on.
7 She pretty soon gave up,

A She seems to be a very nice girl.
B but no one ever came to see me.
C and I got on with things on my own. It was much easier.
D were kept on at expensive private schools.
E Don't you ever want to improve?
F It is never any use to oneself.
G I can't understand a thing.

1	2	3	4	5	6	7

3 Choose the best alternative from the phrasal verbs given to fill in the space provided.

1 I can recall the words you were kind enough to .... to me during our romantic lunch a week ago.
go on ramble on pass on

2 You needn't .... any longer tonight. No need for both of us to be tired tomorrow morning.
stay on drag on get on

3 Charles is .... when most of the summer staff have gone.
got on stayed on kept on

4 Shall we .... with the game now? Ready when you are.
stay on go on drag on

5 But there I go, ... Please forgive me.
rambling on dragging on passing on

6 I .... with my work most weekends.
stay on pass on get on

7 The meeting just .... and on and once again nothing was decided.
rambled on dragged on got on

4 Write the correct form of the appropriate phrasal
verb in the space provided.

1 You would sooner or later be approached and asked if you would like to

.... as a permanent member of the staff.

2 He picked up his pen to .... with his letter.

3 Philip assured her that he had .... the invitation.

4 Without the systematic bombing which took place, the war could have

.... for years.

5 Then she dismissed worry and guilt as self-indulgence and ....
with the business of loving and enjoying him.

6 'You've been very decent to me tonight, letting me .... about
myself.'

7 Some councils make a grant to .... a pupil over 16

.... at school.

5 Write a paragraph on the topic of your choice,
including at least one example of each of the phrasal
verbs you have just studied.

B Progressing

come on   get on   move on   urge on

How's your house coming on¹? When will it be finished?

Oh, yes, Mary is getting on² well. First in her class last week. Clever girl.

It was very clear that the world of the Sixties had moved on, had left him, and most of his world, behind.

The President, reportedly urged on³ by his vice-president, has decided to attend the talks.

'For Heaven's sake ask him how he's getting on with his body building course.'

◆ **LANGUAGE COMMENT**

1 **Come along** means almost the same thing as **come on**.

2 **Get along** means almost the same as **get on**. They are both often used in the continuous tense.

3 **Egg on** and **spur on** mean almost the same as **urge on**.

1 Write the correct phrasal verb to complete the following definitions.

1 If you .... someone .... , you encourage them to do something.

2 If you ask how someone is .... with an activity, you are asking about their progress.

3 If people's ideas, knowledge or beliefs .... , they change and become more modern.

4 If something is .... , it is making progress or developing.

2 Match the sentences and phrases on the left with those on the right.

1 The world moved on and progressed,
2 Murat's not too keen on studying,
3 How is your son getting on at school?
4 Note that California wines

A Well, I wouldn't say he's hopeless, but he has to cheat to come last.
B but time stood still in this little village.
C come on more quickly than their French counterparts.
D he has to be urged on a bit.

1	2	3	4

3 Choose the best alternative from the phrasal verbs given to fill in the space provided.

1 The Count had asked him how he was .... and Tim had said fine.
   moving on   getting on   urging on

2 **Both decisions** .... the Tartars .... to **new forms of protest.**
   got on   came on   urged on

3 The truth is that the world is about to .... from the era where knowledge comes locked up in devices known as books.
   move on   get on   come on

4 Research on this application is .... quite well now.
   moving on   coming on   urging on

4 Write the correct form of the appropriate phrasal verb in the space provided.

1 You should have been .... with your translation in the meantime.

2 I've .... People change in ten years, you know.

3 I am trying to .... him .... to 'try things out for himself'.

4 My new book is .... quite well now.

5 Write a paragraph on the topic of your choice, including at least one example of each of the phrasal verbs you have just studied.

C Beginning

bring on   catch on   come on   move on to

Maman missed dinner because the experience had <u>brought on</u> one of her migraines.

He hasn't really <u>caught on</u>[1] to the system.

It develops most often in the age period between 6 and 10. It can <u>come on</u> quite rapidly, so don't ignore the signs.

The conference was able to <u>move on to</u>[2] other matters of a wider interest.

◆ **LANGUAGE COMMENT**

1 **Cotton on** means almost the same as **catch on**.

2 **Come on to, get on to, go on to, pass on to** and **turn to** mean almost the same as **move on to**.

---

1 Write the correct phrasal verb to complete the following definitions.

1 If a cold, headache, or some other medical condition is .... , it is just starting.

2 If someone .... to something, they understand and learn something.

3 If you .... a particular topic, you bring that topic into a conversation or lecture after you have been talking about something else.

4 Something that .... a bad situation or condition, such as an illness or pain, causes it to occur.

2 Match the phrases on the left with those on the right.

1 If we now move on to voting behaviour
2 The journey had already
3 One of these days he'll
4 I think I've got

A brought on a severe attack of angina.
B a headache coming on.
C the pattern becomes more complicated.
D catch on to what's happening and then we'll be in real trouble.

1	2	3	4

3 Choose the best alternative from the phrasal verbs given to fill in the space provided.

1   The prevalent attitude is to blame technology for having .... the environmental problems we face today.
    caught on   brought on   moved on to

2   At forty that's old age ....
    coming on   moving on to   bringing on

3   We .... the topic of careers.
    came on   caught on   moved on to

4   He'll .... eventually.
    catch on   come on   bring on

4 Write the correct form of the appropriate phrasal verb in the space provided.

1   Let me .... quite a different area.

2   She was feeling sick. It felt like a migraine ....

3   Back strain .... by heavy work may be regarded as an injury.

4   I think she'll .... quickly.

5 Write a paragraph on the topic of your choice, including at least one example of each of the phrasal verbs you have just studied.

D Other meanings

get on go on lay on look on take on

He feels he may have been responsible. He has never got on[1] well with his son and daughter-in-law.

'My dear Pluskat,' he said icily, 'we don't know yet what's going on[2]. We'll let you know when we find out.'

Summerhill children do not go on[3] to be criminals and mobsters after they leave the school.

The organisers had laid on[4] buses to transport people from the city.

He knew I would be able to read them. He could only look on[5] and nod. Because he and his friend were illiterate.

Lord Beaverbrook has taken on a most difficult, delicate, and thankless task.

'I hate to do this, but I've just taken on a huge mortgage.'

◆ **LANGUAGE COMMENT**

1 **Get along** means almost the same as **get on**.

2 **Happen** means almost the same as **go on**.

3 **Move on, press on** and **push on** all have similar meanings. **Go on** is usually followed by the infinitive 'to do' or the preposition 'to'.

4 **Put on** means almost the same as **lay on**.

5 There is also a noun:
   The onlookers just gawped in disbelief.

1 Write the correct phrasal verb to complete the following definitions.

1 If you say that something is .... , you mean that it is taking place at the present time.

2 If you .... to do something, you do it after you have finished something else.

3 If you .... while something happens, you watch it without taking part yourself.

4 If you .... a new job, task or responsibility, you accept it and try to do what is required.

5 If you .... with someone, you like them and have a friendly relationship with them.

6 If you .... something such as food, entertainment, or a service, you provide or supply it.

2 Match the phrases on the left with those on the right.

1 The Indians, indifferent to death,
2 When he had exhausted this interest
3 One of the most astute of Hollywood
   agents
4 Early this evening,
5 You seem to have got on a good deal
   better
6 I spent three weeks down there trying

A the press laid on an informal drinks
   party for us.
B with her than you did last night.
C to figure out what was going on. I still
   don't know.
D just looked on and, I suspect, would
   have let him drown.
E had taken on the job of trying to sell Mr
   Nixon's memoirs.
F would he be able to go on to
   mathematics.

1	2	3	4	5	6

3 Write the correct form of the appropriate phrasal
verb in the space provided.

1 'Let's .... to compare teacher/student ratios and costs in higher
   education.'

2 The first tram service was .... from the Abbey to the Station.

3 There is a great shortage of computer staff and much of the work is

   .... part-time or freelance by married women.

4 The first problem was to find out what was actually ....

5 The person there with whom he .... best was the Count.

6 Your donkeys will be dragged away while you .... , and they
   will not be given back to you.

ON Revision exercises

1 Match the phrasal verbs below to their meanings.

1 get on
2 get on
3 move on to
4 move on
5 take on
6 go on
7 bring on

A when you bring a particular topic into a conversation or lecture after you have been talking about something else

B when you accept a new job, task or responsibility and try to do what is required

C when you like someone and have a friendly relationship with them

D when you start doing or continue doing an activity

E when something causes a bad situation or condition to occur

F when people's ideas, knowledge, or beliefs change and become more modern

G when something is taking place at the present time

1	2	3	4	5	6	7

2 Choose the best alternative from the phrasal verbs given to fill in the space provided.

1 Children are often bored and very frustrated because they are not

.... fast enough with their reading.
bringing on   getting on   rambling on   staying on

2 She .... more work than is good for her.
takes on   gets on   goes on   moves on

3 It had been understood in the family that I would .... to university.
look on   take on   keep on   go on

4 What's .... ? Why is everyone outside?
getting on   going on   dragging on   catching on

5 Another thing, sir. When I was in Pretoria, I didn't .... at all well with this man Muller.
get on   move on   go on   urge on

6 It'll .... his cough again.
urge on   get on   bring on   lay on

7 She is coming over to see us both next week to see how we're

....
staying on   dragging on   getting on   laying on

8   Everybody avoided him when they sensed one of his moods

....

moving on   catching on   rambling on   coming on

9   Can we .... the next point on the agenda?
get on   go on   move on to   lay on

10   He had .... to have a drink.
caught on   brought on   kept on   stayed on

3 Write the letters A, B, or C next to the phrasal verbs
below, according to their meaning. Check your
answers by looking back at page 55. Then use different
colours to highlight each group.

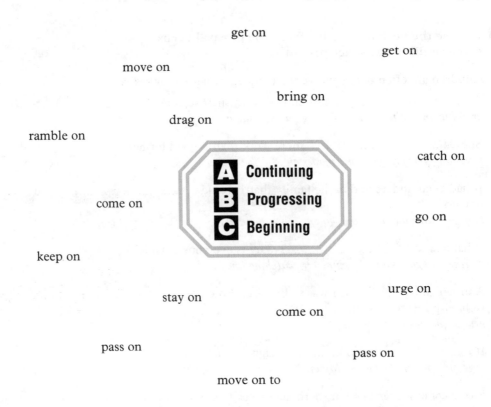

get on

get on

move on

bring on

drag on

ramble on

catch on

A **Continuing**
B **Progressing**
C **Beginning**

come on

go on

keep on

stay on

urge on

come on

pass on

pass on

move on to

OUT

Below are the six most important meanings of OUT and one group of other meanings. In all 44 phrasal verbs have been selected.

Under each of the headings you will see a list of the phrasal verbs you are going to practise. Some verbs appear more than once, as many phrasal verbs have more than one meaning.

You can write other phrasal verbs with the same meaning in the space provided. Use a dictionary if necessary.

A Leaving and Beginning

break out
check out
go out
set out
take out

....
....
....
....

B Removing and Excluding

cancel out   leave out
clean out   opt out
cross out   pull out
get out of   rule out
keep out   talk out of
knock out   throw out

....
....
....
....
....
....
....
....

C Searching and Finding

check out
find out
make out
sound out
try out
turn out
work out

....
....
....
....
....
....

D Producing and Creating

come out
put out
set out
speak out
spell out

....
....
....

E Supporting and Helping

bear out
give out
help out
look out
point out

....
....
....
....
....

F Ending or Disappearing

phase out
run out
sell out
wear out
wipe out

....
....
....
....
....

G Other meanings

carry out
fall out
sort out
stand out
take out on

....
....
....

A   Leaving and Beginning

**break out   check out   go out   set out
take out**

When war <u>*broke out*</u>[1] *my father joined the Navy
and he was drowned at sea.*

She <u>*checked out*</u>[2] *of the hotel and took the train
to Paris.*

I have to <u>*go out*</u>*, I'll be back late tonight.*

Once more they <u>*set out*</u>[3] *to climb the slope of the
mountain.*

Why don't you <u>*take the children out*</u>*?*

'*Can't* <u>*go out*</u> *tonight – my
battery's flat.*'

◆ **LANGUAGE COMMENT**

[1]   There is also a noun:
      ...*a severe* <u>*outbreak*</u> *of food poisoning.*

[2]   **Check in** means the opposite of **check out**.

[3]   **Set off**, **start off** and **start out** mean almost the same as **set out**.
      There is also a noun:
      You should explain this to him at the <u>*outset*</u>*.*

1 Match the sentences and phrases on the left with those
on the right.

1   Billy thanked him and picked up his
    suitcase
2   What time do we have to check out by
    in the morning?
3   He offered to take us out
4   He could not ask her immediately,
5   Would you know what to do if a fire
    broke out in your work place?

A   because she had gone out shopping.
B   Do you have regular fire drill practice?
C   Eleven o'clock, madam.
D   for a drink or something.
E   and set out to walk to The Bell and
    Dragon.

1	2	3	4	5

2 Choose the best alternative from the phrasal verbs
given to fill in the space provided.

1 Immediately an argument .... about the wisdom of the
decision.
set out   went out   broke out

2 If I am to get any sleep I must go, for tomorrow I .... for my
own village before sunrise.
go out   set out   take out

3 It was the first time in my ten years of marriage that I had ....
at night, leaving my husband behind to baby-sit.
gone out   checked out   set out

4 She had .... before I got up. There was no forwarding address.
broken out   checked out   taken out

5 Here in America men were quite obviously .... their entire
families – including the children.
setting out   taking out   breaking out

3 Write the correct form of the appropriate phrasal
verb in the space provided.

1 In the near future, we can expect the same revolt to .... in
other world capitals as well.

2 She had decided to get married and stay in England and not

.... to Africa.

3 I .... Andrea .... to dinner one evening.

4 I got my letters and papers together and .... for the address he
gave me. It wasn't far.

5 'We'll be .... tomorrow. Could you have our bill ready, please?'

4 Write a paragraph on the topic of your choice,
including at least one example of each of the phrasal
verbs you have just studied.

Bad Jokes

4 Find the logical ending for each of the jokes beginning
on the left.

1   What did one candle say to the other
candle?
2   Where do cows go for a night out?
3   Why did the banana go out with the
prune?
4   Mother, you promised to take me out to
see the monkeys.
5   Most women set out to try to change a
man,

A   He couldn't find a date.
B   To the moo-ooo-vies.
C   Are you going out tonight?
D   Johnny, why do you want to go out to
see the monkeys when your little
brothers are here?
E   and when they have changed him they
do not like him.

1	2	3	4	5

5 Write a paragraph on the topic of your choice,
including at least one example of each of the phrasal
verbs you have just studied.

B Removing and Excluding   Part 1

cancel out   clean out   cross out   get out of   keep out   knock out

The drug produces side effects, tending to cancel out *the benefits.*

I spent three days cleaning our flat out[1].

You haven't got time to rewrite it, just cross out[2] *clearly what you want to change and write it above.*

I think they're trying to get out of[3] *their obligations under the agreement.*

They had a guard dog to keep out *intruders.*

Their aim is for the Social Democrats to knock out *the Labour Party.*

◆ LANGUAGE COMMENT

1 **Clear out** means almost the same as **clean out**.

2 **Delete** means almost the same as **cross out**.

3 This is an informal use. **Wriggle out of** means almost the same as **get out of**.

1 Write the correct phrasal verb to complete the following definitions.

1 If one thing .... another thing .... or if two things ....

each other .... , they have opposite effects, so that when they are combined no real effect is produced.

2 To .... someone or something .... of a place means to prevent them from entering it or being there.

3 If you .... doing something, you avoid doing it.

2 Match the sentences and phrases on the left with those on the right.

1 Fascism seems to be spreading here.
2 The explosion hurt no one,
3 Why on earth are you going, then?
4 It's not worth doing a draft during an exam,
5 Increased productivity and generous staffing could be said
6 The garage is a mess again.

A to cancel each other out.
B just cross it out and rewrite it above.
C except that it knocked out Colonel Lacour.
D I'll have to clean it out next weekend.
E It's too late to get out of it.
F We have got to keep crazy 'isms' out of our country.

1	2	3	4	5	6

3 Choose the best alternative from the phrasal verbs
given to fill in the space provided.

1 I would promptly write it down and then .... it .... again.
cross out   keep out   cancel out

2 To .... intruders every inch of this labyrinth was mined.
cross out   keep out   clean out

3 The one effect tends to .... the other ....
cancel out   cross out   get out of

4 He made me fill a form in. And there was no way I could .... it.
keep out   get out of   cross out

5 Regularly .... food cupboards.
keep out   clean out   cancel out

6 The tablet had .... her .... for four hours.
crossed out   cleaned out   knocked out

4 Write the correct form of the appropriate phrasal
verb in the space provided.

1 I had to massage the wound and .... it .... every day.

2 I couldn't .... writing the script, I was contractually
committed.

3 Now and then he frowned, ... something .... and rewrote it.

4 Noise would be reduced but this would be .... by extra traffic
at Luton airport.

5 Almost 2000 tanks had been .... of action by missiles.

6 The curtains did not .... the diffused lamplight from the street
below.

B Removing and Excluding   Part 2

leave out   opt out   pull out   rule out   talk out of   throw out

One or two scenes in the play were <u>left out</u>[1] of the performance.

He tried to <u>opt out</u> of political and economic decision-making.

We've invested too much money and manpower to <u>pull out</u> now.

They can't <u>rule out</u>[2] the possibility that he was kidnapped.

He tried to <u>talk me out of</u>[3] buying such a big car.

I can remember my parents <u>throwing out</u>[4] their old furniture.

◆ **LANGUAGE COMMENT**

[1] **Miss out** means almost the same as **leave out**.

[2] **Dismiss** means almost the same as **rule out**.

[3] **Talk into** means the opposite of **talk out of**.

[4] **Throw away** means almost the same as **throw out**.

1 **Match the phrases on the left with those on the right.**

1 It's no use trying to talk me out of it,
2 Her parents threw her out
3 Police have ruled out murder
4 Hospitals are opting out
5 I shan't be available,
6 You have to pay a 10% deposit

A of health authority control.
B so you will have to leave me out.
C I've made up my mind.
D when they found she was pregnant.
E but are still holding several people for questioning.
F which you lose if you pull out.

1	2	3	4	5	6

2 **Choose the best alternative from the phrasal verbs given to fill in the space provided.**

1 I spent the whole of last night trying to .... her .... resigning.
opt out   talk out of   pull out

2 I knew that if I didn't do the work pretty quickly I'd be ....
and replaced.
opted out   thrown out   talked out of

3 There were many people who had .... of the rat race.
opted out   thrown out   left out

4 A search had .... the possibility of further bombs.
pulled out   thrown out   ruled out

5   I'm aware that we've had to .... much interesting and important work.
    leave out   opt out   talk out of

6   Troops had begun to .... of the area.
    pull out   leave out   rule out

3 Write the correct form of the appropriate phrasal verb in the space provided.

1   Washington need not .... a selective military aid program.

2   He .... his party .... of the coalition.

3   Today there is a growing tendency for people to ....

4   New societies may be tempted to .... the principles of democracy.

5   She managed to .... herself .... going.

6   Just go through it and check that you haven't .... anything ....

Bad Jokes

4 Find the logical ending for each of the jokes beginning on the left.

1   Is it true my baby brother came from Heaven?
2   Why was Cinderella thrown out of the England football team?
3   Why was your brother thrown out of the submarine service?
4   Why did a man throw his watch out of the window?

A   To see time fly.
B   Yes, and I don't blame God for throwing him out.
C   Because she kept running away from the ball.
D   He liked to sleep with the windows open.

1	2	3	4

C Searching and Finding

check out find out make out sound out try out turn out work out

It might be difficult to transfer your money, so <u>check it out</u> with the manager.

I'm only interested in <u>finding out</u>[1] what the facts are.

It is sometimes difficult to <u>make out</u> what is said over an airport loudspeaker.

Kids at school were always <u>sounding her out</u> about their chances of being moved to the top of the list.

Oxford is <u>trying out</u> another idea to help working parents.

It may look true in the short run and <u>turn out</u> to be false in the longer run.

We are always hopeful that a more peaceful solution can be <u>worked out</u>[2].

'Well, it's going fine at the moment, but if they ever <u>find out</u> we're chocolate coated with a minty centre we could be in big trouble.'

◆ **LANGUAGE COMMENT**

1 **Discover** means almost the same as **find out**.

2 **Figure out** means almost the same as **work out**.

1 Write the correct phrasal verb to complete the following definitions.

1 If you .... someone ...., you ask them questions in order to find out their views, especially about what should or will happen in a particular situation.

2 If something or someone .... to be a particular thing, they are discovered to be that thing.

3 If you .... a solution or a plan, you think about it carefully and find a solution or decide what to do.

4 If you can .... something ...., you manage to see or hear it.

5 If you .... something .... , you find out about it or examine it because you want to make sure that everything is correct or safe.

2 **Match the phrases on the left with those on the right.**

1 She felt sheer terror	A before we buy it.
2 Frank was going to check out the restaurant floor	B turn out to be dysentery or paratyphoid infections.
3 I'm going to lose my French passport,	C until she made out Tim's friendly wave and heard his voice calling.
4 Some epidemics of intestinal flu	D who have been sounded out on the subject suggested your name.
5 All the members of the English Department	E unless I can work something out.
6 Let's try it out	F to see whether anything unusual was going on.
7 We found out	G that she was wrong.

1	2	3	4	5	6	7

3 **Choose the best alternative from the phrasal verbs given to fill in the space provided.**

1 Could you .... the appointments for my trip next week?
sound out   try out   check out

2 We're .... it .... at the moment, but we haven't had any feedback yet.
trying out   turning out   making out

3 I .... the train times.
found out   turned out   made out

4 We could begin to .... the best ways to help these youngsters.
make out   turn out   work out

5 He could .... the spires of Notre Dame across the miles of roofs.
make out   find out   turn out

6 Standard Oil's officials were .... by Conoco's investment banker.
made out   sounded out   worked out

7 This may not seem particularly earthshaking, but it could ....
to be one of the most momentous developments of the decade.
sound out   try out   turn out

4 Write the correct form of the appropriate phrasal
verb in the space provided.

1 Those people who have been .... on this were, on the whole,
favourable.

2 A police officer would be .... the statement Mrs Mossman had
just made.

3 The Marvin's house .... to be an old converted barn.

4 It's best to .... this .... first on a bit of
spare fabric.

5 Can you .... how much it costs?

6 I stopped and sat down to .... where I would go next.

7 He could just .... the number plate of the car.

5 Find the logical ending for each of the jokes beginning
on the left.

1 What is ignorance?
2 Do you think insects have brains?
3 Why did the girl rhino paint her head
  yellow?
4 The Texan turned out to be good-
  natured, generous and likeable.
5 Modesty is the art of encouraging
  people
6 I have found that the best way to give
  advice to your children is

A to find out for themselves how
  wonderful you are.
B In three days no one could stand him.
C Yes, they soon work out where we're
  holding our picnic.
D to find out what they want and then
  advise them to do it.
E When you don't know something and
  somebody finds out.
F She wanted to find out if blondes have
  more fun.

1	2	3	4	5	6

D Producing and Creating

come out put out set out speak out spell out

Remember this report <u>came out</u>[1] after the election.

The World Wildlife Fund <u>put out</u>[2] a press release.

Operating instructions are clearly <u>set out</u>[3] at the side of most public telephones.

He <u>spoke out</u> early against the war in Vietnam.

The first person to <u>spell this out</u> clearly was Alvin Toffler in his book 'Future Shock'.

◆ **LANGUAGE COMMENT**

1 **Appear** means almost the same as **come out**.

2 **Issue** means almost the same as **put out**.

3 **Lay out** means almost the same as **set out**.

1 Write the correct phrasal verb to complete the following definitions.

1 If you .... something .... , you explain it in detail or in a very clear way.

2 If you .... , you express your views forcefully and publicly, especially in order to criticize or oppose something.

3 If a statement or story is .... , it is officially told to people.

4 If you .... facts, ideas, or opinions, you explain them in writing or in speech in a clear and organized way.

5 When something such as a book .... , it is published or becomes available to the public.

2 Match the sentences and phrases on the left with those on the right.

1 I'm afraid I don't understand.
2 The book came out first in Germany
3 The story that the committee will put out
4 She did not speak out
5 The proposed project must be detailed,

A in condemnation of the massacre.
B where it has sold 160,000 copies.
C Let me spell it out for you – you're fired.
D with all its stages set out carefully.
E has nothing to do with the truth.

1	2	3	4	5

3 Choose the best alternative from the phrasal verbs given to fill in the space provided.

1 He .... against racial discrimination many times.
set out   put out   spoke out

2 He asked me to send him any new stamps which might ....
come out   speak out   put out

3 This is .... in the critical writings of the American art world.
spoken out   spelled out   come out

4 He .... a statement denouncing the commission's conclusions.
spoke out   came out   put out

5 Let us proceed to the results. They are .... below in Table 3.3.
put out   set out   spoken out

4 Write the correct form of the appropriate phrasal verb in the space provided.

1 Important aspects of the cost of studying in Britain are ....
here: tuition fees and living expenses.

2 Various scare stories have been .... during the last few years.

3 It seems only yesterday that Opus 100 .... , and now he's past the halfway mark of his second symphony.

4 Garrett wouldn't dare .... against Byrne.

5 Let me try and .... what I mean by that.

5 Write a paragraph on the topic of your choice, including at least one example of each of the phrasal verbs you have just studied.

E Supporting and Helping

**bear out   give out   help out   look out
point out**

She provided a strong counter-argument, with some witnesses to <u>bear her out</u>.

They also <u>give out</u>[1] information about courses for teachers of English.

Neighbourhood associations <u>help out</u> the poor with funeral expenses.

'<u>Look out</u>[2],' I said. 'There's someone coming.'

Critics were quick to <u>point out</u> the weaknesses in these arguments.

◆ LANGUAGE COMMENT

1 **Hand out** and **pass out** mean almost the same as **give out**.
A **handout** is a document which gives information about something
and is given to people free.

2 **Watch out** and **mind out** mean almost the same as **look out**.

1 Write the correct phrasal verb to complete the
following definitions.

1 You say or shout .... to warn someone that they are in danger.

2 If you .... someone .... , you do them a
favour, such as lending them money or doing some of their work.

3 If someone or something .... what you are saying, they support
what you are saying.

4 If you .... something .... , you give
people an important piece of information or correct their mistaken ideas.

2 Match the sentences and phrases on the left with those
on the right.

1 Look out.
2 Come back at the end of the week if
   you're still short of money
3 The machine did not in fact bear out
4 She pointed out
5 Some employers give out a lot of
   information.

A Others refuse to part with any.
B the claims made for it.
C and I'll see if I can help you out.
D There's someone coming.
E that he was wrong.

1	2	3	4	5

3 Choose the best alternative from the phrasal verbs given to fill in the space provided.

1 I .... this .... to you in a letter last week.
   bore out pointed out gave out

2 The claims are not .... by the evidence.
   borne out given out looked out

3 Someone saw the second hand-grenade and said : '..........................., he's got another'.
   Help out Look out Point out

4 My parents .... us .... when Bruno was born.
   bore out gave out helped out

5 'I'm sorry; we're not permitted to .... that information.' Miss Young was polite but firm.
   bear out point out give out

4 Write the correct form of the appropriate phrasal verb in the space provided.

1 'It's a golden opportunity, really,' Johnson ....

2 '..........................., I'm going to drop a rock,' I shouted.

3 Howard .... drinks to his guests.

4 She .... with the instruction.

5 . . . and, Gill, perhaps you'll .... me .... on this, we got very similar results to Hobson's.

5 Write a paragraph on the topic of your choice, including at least one example of each of the phrasal verbs you have just studied.

F Ending or Disappearing

phase out run out sell out wear out wipe out

Gold has been phased out of the monetary system.

We were rapidly running out of money.

Shops almost immediately sold out of the advertised goods.

Visitors wear us out[1] more than the children do.

Epidemics wiped out[2] the local population.

◆ **LANGUAGE COMMENT**

1 **Exhaust** and **tire out** mean almost the same as **wear out**.

2 **Eradicate** is a more formal word for **wipe out**.

1 **Match the sentences and phrases on the left with those on the right.**

1 Can I use your lighter?
2 That isn't show jumping.
3 We can't just change over to the new system tomorrow.
4 Could I buy some sun cream?
5 He was determined to wipe out

A We'll have to phase the old one out as we train people.
B the memory of his years in prison.
C I've run out of matches.
D It's a marathon designed to wear the horse out.
E Sorry, we've sold out.

1	2	3	4	5

2 **Choose the best alternative from the phrasal verbs given to fill in the space provided.**

1 Did you get it? No, they'd .... by the time I got there.
wiped out   phased out   sold out

2 There's no point in .... yourself ....
wearing out   running out   phasing out

3 What did you do when you .... of toilet paper?
wore out   wiped out   ran out

4   Many tribes were .... by contact with European settlers.
    phased out   sold out   wiped out

5   I think we should .... it .... over a
    two-year period.
    phase out   run out   wear out

3 Write the correct form of the appropriate phrasal
    verb in the space provided.

1   This type of weapon was now being finally ....

2   They planned one big assault to .... the remains of the ghetto.

3   I'm sorry we've .... of that particular brand.

4   It looks as if oil will .... faster than coal.

5   They .... us .... with their constant
    screaming and crying.

4 Write a paragraph on the topic of your choice,
    including at least one example of each of the phrasal
    verbs you have just studied.

G Other meanings

**carry out fall out sort out stand out
take out on**

*The first experiments were <u>carried out</u> by Dr Preston
McLendon.*

*She had <u>fallen out</u> so severely with her parents that she
couldn't go home.*

*It was an intelligence test, intended to <u>sort out</u> the
children capable of attempting the papers.*

*The Australian tour <u>stands out</u> as the most satisfying
and enjoyable of them all.*

*I was in a depressed and hostile mood, needing to
<u>take my bad feelings out on</u> someone.*

*'Understaffed!!! – I've <u>carried
out</u> five operations this morning
and I'm only the janitor!'*

1 **Write the correct phrasal verb to complete the
following definitions.**

1 If you .... something .... someone, you
behave in an unpleasant way towards them because you feel angry or upset.

2 If something .... from other things of the same kind, it is much
better or much more important than those other things.

3 If you .... with someone, you have an argument and are no
longer friendly with them.

4 If you .... a group of things, you consider them carefully and
divide them into categories that are clearly different from each other.

5 If you .... a task, you do it.

2 **Write the correct form of the appropriate phrasal
verb in the space provided.**

1 It was the only time we ever .... , in all those years together.

2 She .... most of her unhappiness ....
her husband.

3 He gave guarantees that such a policy will be .... if his Party
achieves office.

4 The remaining girls were collecting and .... the balls.

5 This is one of the things that .... in my memory.

●●●

OUT Revision exercises

1 Choose the best alternative from the phrasal verbs
given to fill in the space provided.

1 It took quite a while to .... all our luggage.
fall out   sort out   bear out   keep out

2 When the book .... , I was very anxious to know about sales.
came out   put out   cleaned out   broke out

3 Martha and Wilf's mother .... at Lily's wedding and they
haven't spoken since.
spoke out   bore out   crossed out   fell out

4 Measles had .... in the village.
broken out   come out   checked out   set out

5 Do not .... these .... as gimmicks: they
are very useful.
carry out   rule out   sound out   work out

6 I think it was .... quite clearly in the report.
helped out   spelled out   spoken out   gone out

7 We cannot prove that what we know is true, and it may ....
to be false.
sound out   pull out   turn out   take out

8 Neither Asquith nor Grey .... in public to clear Haldane's
name.
spelled out   looked out   pointed out   spoke out

9 I was .... my desk at the office on my last day there.
cleaning out   selling out   knocking out   trying out

10 'Woman' magazine has just .... a survey.
carried out   opted out   spoke out   broke out

11 Mr Dekker and his son .... to walk to Whitelake River.
set out   put out   got out of   kept out

12 Hospitals are .... of health authority control.
phasing out   making out   opting out   putting out

13 Mr Merrit .... this problem .... to you
the other day.
wiped out   wore out   put out   pointed out

14 Should I .... it .... and wash the pot?
rule out   find out   opt out   throw out

15 The little money she had was .... and she had herself and two children to keep.
checking out   turning out   running out   putting out

16 We'll do anything to .... work.
talk out of   fall out   get out of   bear out

17 Faye Seidel .... her husband .... his plan.
got out of   talked out of   threw out   sorted out

18 You used to .... me .... to shows.
give out   wipe out   take out   check out

19 We can't .... Uncle Jack .... We've invited the whole family apart from him.
wipe out   sound out   leave out   carry out

20 First of all, we have to .... how much it costs. Phone them up and ask.
try out   break out   put out   find out

21 Harris's assertion is hardly .... by the facts.
spoken out   fallen out   knocked out   borne out

22 Economists have tried to .... an alternative economic system.
find out   work out   clean out   sell out

2 Write the letters D or E next to each phrasal verb depending on which of the two groups each belongs to. Check your answers by looking at page 67.

OVER

Below are the two most important meanings of OVER and one group of other meanings. In all 13 phrasal verbs have been selected.

Under each of the headings you will see a list of the phrasal verbs you are going to practise.

You can write other phrasal verbs with the same meaning in the space provided. Use a dictionary if necessary.

A Considering and Communicating

look over
put over
talk over
think over

....

....

....

....

....

....

....

B Changing and Transferring

change over
hand over
take over (two meanings)
win over

....

....

....

....

....

....

C Other meanings

get over with
pass over
run over
smooth over

....

....

....

....

....

....

A Considering and Communicating

look over put over talk over think over

Sometimes he would <u>look over</u> the article I had written, shrug, and tear it up.

The university's prospectuses didn't <u>put it over</u>[1] the way I wanted to.

I'll <u>talk it over</u> with Len tonight and let you know tomorrow.

He said he would leave me alone to <u>think things over</u>[2] for five minutes.

◆ **LANGUAGE COMMENT**

[1] **Put across, get across** and **get over** all have similar meanings.

[2] **Chew over, mull over** and **turn over** mean almost the same as **think over; consider** is a slightly more formal word.

1 Write the correct phrasal verb to complete the following definitions.

1 When you .... an idea .... , you succeed in describing or explaining it to someone.

2 If you .... something .... , you discuss it with someone.

3 If you .... someone or something .... , you examine or inspect them in order to get a general idea of what they are like.

4 If you .... something .... , you consider it carefully before making a decision.

2 Match the sentences and phrases on the left with those on the right.

1 How did the philosopher manage to get the elephant across the Atlantic without using a boat or plane?

2 There's plenty of opportunity for you

3 With the modern resources available,

4 If you're worried,

A get the vet to look it over.
B He just thought it over.
C you can put a message over nationally or world-wide.
D to talk your problems over with someone.

1	2	3	4

3 Choose the best alternative from the phrasal verbs
given to fill in the space provided.

1 He knew she was busy .... him .... , but he didn't turn round.
talking over   looking over   putting over

2 I agreed to go home and .... things .... with my father.
talk over   put over   think over

3 Take your time. .... it .... for a few days, but I think it's a great
opportunity.
Talk over   Put over   Think over

4 There are enough of them to .... their point of view.
think over   look over   put over

4 Write the correct form of the appropriate phrasal
verb in the space provided.

1 How to .... it .... to the class, that's the trouble.

2 We all met in Pat's room, to .... what we had seen.

3 He was called in to .... the bomb damage to the House of
Commons.

4 When a person tells you, 'I'll .... it .... and let you know' – you
know.

5 Write a paragraph on the topic of your choice,
including at least one example of each of the phrasal
verbs you have just studied.

B Changing and Transferring

change over   hand over   take over   win over

They had been Socialist till several years ago, then they changed over[1] to Conservative.

Sir John handed over to his deputy and left.

Some people wanted to take over[2] my father's oil importing business.

He was 'Jacko' Reed, a former rugby star who had recently taken over as manager of the bank's main branch in the city.

Local radio stations have done their best to win over[3] new audiences.

◆ LANGUAGE COMMENT

1 **Go over, move over** and **switch over** have similar meanings.
There is also a noun:
The changeover took place at Easter.

2 There is also a noun:
The trend towards takeovers has intensified.

3 **Win round** means almost the same as **win over**.

1 Write the correct phrasal verb to complete the following definitions.

1 If you .... to someone, you give them the responsibility for dealing with a particular situation or problem.

2 If you .... a job or a responsibility, you start doing it or being responsible for it after someone else has finished.

3 If you .... someone .... , you persuade them to support you or agree with you.

4 To .... from one thing to another means to stop doing or using one thing and change to something else.

5 To .... a company or a country means to gain control of it.

2 Match the phrases on the left with those on the right.

1 Most smokers have changed over
2 Well-trained and equipped troops
3 A new chairman or managing director who has just taken over
4 I was completely won over
5 Children are often handed over

A could probably take over the country.
B isn't too familiar with the procedures.
C by the courtesy and direct simplicity of the people.
D to a milder cigarette.
E to the child-minder at seven a.m.

1	2	3	4	5

3 Choose the best alternative from the phrasal verbs given to fill in the space provided.

1 Thornaby .... as secretary in 1976.
won over   took over   changed over

2 We began to .... a sizeable number of members to our cause.
take over   hand over   win over

3 The agency has advised its clients to .... or merge with another company.
take over   change over   win over

4 We've just .... our computer system .... to IBM.
taken over   won over   changed over

5 I will willingly retire from this investigation and .... it ....
hand over   change over   take over

4 Write the correct form of the appropriate phrasal verb in the space provided.

1 The I.P.C. was .... by the huge Reed Paper Group.

2 We should consider .... from electricity to gas: it's so much cheaper.

3 She gave a short welcoming speech and .... to her assistant.

4 Benn had succeeded in .... those in authority to the workers' cause.

5 When the insects .... the world, we hope they will remember with gratitude how we took them along on all our picnics.

C   Other meanings

**get over with   pass over
run over   smooth over**

*Let's try and get this meeting over
with as quickly as possible.*

*Neither of us got the job. We were
both passed over[1] in mysterious
circumstances.*

*The sweat rolled down my neck, and
we almost ran over[2] some little animal
or other that was crossing the road.*

*She tried to smooth over the
differences between them.*

*'The practice of astrology took a major step
toward achieving credibility today when, as
predicted, everyone born under the sign of
Scorpio was run over by an egg lorry.'*

◆ **LANGUAGE COMMENT**

1 This meaning of **pass over** is always passive. **Be rejected** means
almost the same as **be passed over**.

2 **Run down, knock down** and **knock over** mean almost the same as
run over.

1 Write the correct phrasal verb to complete the
following definitions.

1   If you are .... for a job or position that you are trying to get, it
is given to someone who is less well-qualified or experienced than you.

2   If a vehicle .... someone or something, it hits them or drives
over them causing injury or damage.

3   If you .... something .... , you do and complete something
unpleasant that must be done.

4   If you .... a problem or a difficulty, you talk about it in a way
that makes it seem less serious and easier to deal with.

2 Match the phrases on the left with those on the right.

1 What would happen if I were to become ill
2 He was grateful for her help in smoothing over
3 He wanted to get this miserable business over with
4 Cindy knew why she had been passed over;

A what could have become an embarrassing scene.
B she was not important enough.
C as quickly as possible.
D or get run over by a bus?

1	2	3	4

3 Write the correct form of the appropriate phrasal verb in the space provided.

1 Give Woods his final warning now and .... it ....

2 I tried to .... the awkwardness of this first meeting.

3 He was completely out of control and narrowly avoided .... a group of pedestrians.

4 Arnold had recently been .... for promotion.

Bad Jokes

4 Find the logical ending for each of the jokes beginning on the left.

1 Is your sister a bad driver?
2 I'm not a fighter, I have bad reflexes.
3 I'm very sorry, but I've just run over your cat. I'd like to replace it.

A I was once run over by a car being pushed by two guys.
B How good are you at catching mice?
C Well, every time she goes out in the car, Dad puts a glass panel in the floor so that she can see who she's run over.

1	2	3

OVER Revision exercises

1 Choose the best alternative from the phrasal verbs
given to fill in the space provided.

1 No tycoon has ever been able to .... it ....
win over   run over   take over   look over

2 He got it into his head he was being .... for promotion.
passed over   got over with   smoothed over   taken over

3 Someone had to try and .... things .... between them.
run over   put over   take over   smooth over

4 Can we just .... this questioning ....?
talk over   get over with   win over   think over

5 It is difficult for her to .... her own thoughts.
put over   get over with   change over   hand over

6 I wanted to .... one or two business problems which we had
discussed.
win over   think over   change over   get over with

2 Complete the phrasal verbs given in the two meanings
illustrated below. Check your answers on page 87.

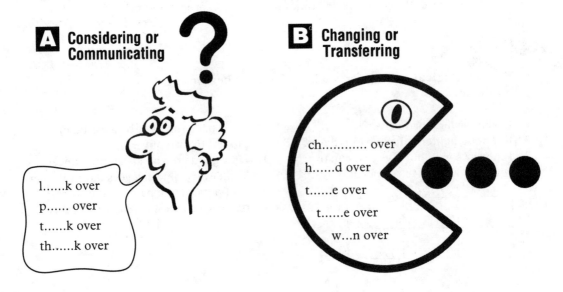

A Considering or
Communicating

l......k over
p...... over
t......k over
th......k over

B Changing or
Transferring

ch............ over
h......d over
t......e over
t......e over
w...n over

UP

Below are the seven most important meanings of UP and one group of other meanings. In all 65 phrasal verbs have been selected.

Under each of the headings you will see a list of the phrasal verbs which you are going to practise. Some verbs appear more than once, as many phrasal verbs have more than one meaning.

You can write other phrasal verbs with the same meaning in the space provided. Use a dictionary if necessary.

A Increasing and Improving

back up	grow up
bring up	pick up
brush up	push up
build up	save up
cheer up	speak up
do up	(two meanings)
dress up	speed up
go up	stir up

....

....

....

....

B Preparing

draw up	soften up
fix up	warm up
set up	

....

....

C Approaching

catch up
come up against
face up to
keep up
live up to

....

....

....

E Completing and Finishing

check up	give up
clear up	pull up
(two meanings)	sum up
cover up	tidy up
do up	use up
drink up	weigh up
end up	wind up
follow up	

....

....

....

F Happening and Creating

bring up
come up
come up with
make up
pick up (two meanings)
think up
turn up

....

....

....

....

D Disrupting and Damaging

blow up	mess up
break up	mix up
hold up	slip up

....

....

G Collecting and Being together

look up	put up
make up	take up on
pick up	

....

....

....

H Other meanings

look up	take up
make up for	turn up
put up with	

....

....

....

A Increasing and Improving Part 1

back up bring up brush up build up
cheer up do up dress up go up

The more bills you can include to back up[1] your claim, the happier the finance department will be.

I brought up two children alone.

I need to brush up my English: I haven't used it for seven years.

We helped to build up the wealth of this country.

Her friends tried to cheer her up, telling her she wasn't missing much.

They wanted payment in cash for doing up[2] the kitchen of one of his cottages.

Rather than sit at home, they all get dressed up and go out.

The price of petrol and oil related products will go up steadily.

"Mine too – every week it's 'meat's gone up' – 'clothing's gone up' – 'rent's going up' . . ."

◆ **LANGUAGE COMMENT**

1 **Support** means almost the same as back up.
There is also a noun:
...the tremendous computer back-up which each mission required.

2 **Renovate** is a more formal word for **do up**.

1 Match the sentences and phrases on the left with those on the right.

1 Body temperature doesn't stay fixed at 98.4 F.
2 If too much pressure builds up,
3 Another mistake.
4 She bought strawberries
5 We should back up the system every evening,
6 Fathers are beginning to play a bigger role
7 The theatre was horrible,
8 She was glad that she was all dressed up

A in bringing up children, with benefits to everyone.
B You need to brush up your shorthand.
C to cheer herself up.
D It is always going up and down a little, depending on the time of day.
E and had done her hair that morning.
F done up as cheaply as possible.
G if not we risk losing a lot of data.
H it will explode.

1	2	3	4	5	6	7	8

2 Choose the best alternative from the phrasal verbs given to fill in the space provided.

1 The cost of the thing you want to buy can have .... a lot by the time you have saved enough to pay for it.
built up gone up brought up

2 Their demands for independence were .... with quotes from western political writers.
backed up brushed up cheered up

3 His organizational knowledge and personal reputation has .... the business
....
cheered up done up built up

4 Why don't we buy some flowers to .... the place .... a bit?
build up cheer up dress up

5 We're going to buy a small cottage in the country to .... when we retire.
do up build up go up

6 I can't be bothered to .... this evening.
cheer up dress up brush up

7 I've got a four-year-old son to .... on my own.
build up bring up brush up

8 I would like to .... my zoology.
dress up brush up back up

3 Write the correct form of the appropriate phrasal verb in the space provided.

1 You can make quite a lot of money .... old properties.

2 These were the children who had been properly .... without parental lies and lectures.

3 When you go shopping all you hear is how everything has ....

4 She helped them to .... their French.

5 This claim is .... by the fact that every year more and more money is being spent on arms.

6 We're trying to .... a collection of herbs and spices.

7 I never get .... when I'm invited somewhere, I always go as I am.

8 .... ! It's not the end of the world, you know.

A   Increasing and Improving   Part 2

**grow up   pick up   push up   save up
speak up   speed up   stir up**

*Children should <u>grow up</u> with a fond attitude towards
all humanity.*

The economy is <u>picking up</u>[1].

*The Bank of Japan rightly judged that it was too
early to <u>push up</u> interest rates to defend the yen.*

They're <u>saving up</u> money for a holiday.

Could you please <u>speak up</u>. We can't hear you at the back.

Never be frightened of <u>speaking up</u> for your beliefs.

*Bad housing and poverty <u>speed up</u>[2] the breakdown
of family life.*

*He was prevented from speaking on the grounds
that it would <u>stir up</u>[3] trouble.*

*'Since my prayers are taking such an
inordinately long time to get
answered, I wondered if it would
<u>speed things up</u> if you took me on
privately?'*

◆ **LANGUAGE COMMENT**

1 **Look up** means almost the same as **pick up,** but it is more informal.

2 **Accelerate** is a more formal word for **speed up.**

3 **Provoke** and **incite** are more formal words for **stir up.**

1 Match the sentences and phrases on the left with those
on the right.

1 The players themselves should speak up
2 Second, the institutions have been accused of
3 You can do some slower movements,
4 She was one of those people
5 The relatives will save up
6 What do you want to be
7 Retail demand for diamonds has
8 If you don't speak up,

A then speed them up a bit.
B when you grow up?
C picked up in recent weeks.
D in favour of non-racial cricket.
E pushing up land prices.
F they won't be able to hear you.
G who likes stirring things up.
H to put a child through secondary school.

1	2	3	4	5	6	7	8

2 Choose the best alternative from the phrasal verbs
given to fill in the space provided.

1 They're a long way ahead of us. .... !
   Speed up   Save up   Go up

2 Why do they not .... for themselves?
   pick up   push up   speak up

3 They .... in the early days of television.
   grew up   pushed up   picked up

4 A rally was called to .... popular support for nuclear
   disarmament.
   grow up   stir up   speak up

5 If you want to buy something that expensive, you have to ....
   stir up   pick up   save up

6 ...techniques which .... the temperature .... to 200°C.
   pick up   speak up   push up

7 You have to .... , to project your voice to the back of the room.
   stir up   speak up   speed up

8 People like her are waiting for trade to ....
   pick up   grow up   save up

3 Write the correct form of the appropriate phrasal
verb in the space provided.

1 We seem to have a bad line. Could you .... , please?

2 The new procedures are designed to .... the processing of
   insurance claims.

3 Business should .... after the election.

4 She needed someone to .... for her.

5 It'll take me at least a year to .... for a new guitar.

6 ... a crazy scheme to corner the champagne market with a view to
   .... the price and making a huge profit.

7 I've lived in London for seven years, but I .... in Newcastle.

8 Being back in the hospital .... unpleasant memories.

B Preparing

draw up fix up set up soften up warm up

The committee _drew up_[1] a
five-point plan to revive
the economy.

Have you done anything
about _fixing up_[2] a meeting
place?

The first thing to do in a crisis is to
set up a committee.

I wondered if there was any
hope of _softening him up_[3]?

Shall we have a game
straight away, or would you
rather _warm up_[4] first?

'You Christians think
you're unlucky ...
I'm the _warm-up_
man!'

◆ **LANGUAGE COMMENT**

1 **Formulate** is a formal word for **draw up**.

2 **Arrange** is a more formal word for **fix up**; **line up** means almost the
same.

3 **Butter up** and **sweeten up** mean almost the same as **soften up**.

4 **Limber up** and **loosen up** mean almost the same as **warm up**.
There is also a noun and an adjective:
During the warm-up exercises, I was still shaking.

1 Write the correct phrasal verb to complete the following definitions.

1 If you .... something .... , you make the arrangements that are
necessary to achieve it.

2 When you .... a document, list, or plan, you prepare it and
write it out.

3 If you .... someone .... , you praise them or try to please them
because you want to ask them to do something for you which they do not really want
to do.

4 If you .... something .... , you make the arrangements and
preparations that are necessary for it to start.

2 Match the sentences and phrases on the left with those
on the right.

1 Could you draw up a list
2 You can ask Jane
3 She is warming up on another court,
4 The school used to lack formal links
   with industry.
5 The Ambassador is also trying to soften
   up Velasco

A to fix up a taxi for you.
B on the Cuban problem.
C Now we have set them up at every
   level.
D of what we need to buy next year?
E preparing for the most important match
   of her career.

1	2	3	4	5

3 Choose the best alternative from the phrasal verbs
given to fill in the space provided.

1 It took a long time to .... the experiment.
   draw up   warm up   set up

2 The holiday is all .... you'll be pleased to hear.
   fixed up   drawn up   warmed up

3 We'll have to .... him .... first, before we ask for a new computer.
   fix up   soften up   draw up

4 A charter was .... , setting out their policies.
   warmed up   softened up   drawn up

5 I always spend ten minutes .... before a race.
   drawing up   softening up   warming up

4 Write the correct form of the appropriate phrasal
verb in the space provided.

1 They had been trained in a special school .... by Brigadier
   James Gavin.

2 We'll .... a nice meal for the three of us.

3 The plan of action for the forthcoming election had been ....
   months in advance.

4 They jogged around the track twice to ....

5 She's .... me .... for something: I wish I knew what it was.

C Approaching

**catch up   come up against   face up to   keep up
live up to**

She stood still, allowing him to catch her up.

*The first time I did this I came up against[1] an
unforeseen problem.*

*Issues like these simply cannot be ignored; the
problems have to be faced up to.*

*Penny tended to work through her lunch hour
in an effort to keep up with her work*

The film didn't live up to[2] my expectations.

'*I'm sorry, J.B., the Company feels that you
have failed to live up to the desk.*'

◆ **LANGUAGE COMMENT**

1 **Run up against** means almost the same as
come up against.

2 **Measure up to** and **match up to** mean almost the same as **live up to**.

1 Write the correct phrasal verb to complete the
following definitions.

1 If you .... a difficult situation, you accept it and deal with it.

2 If someone or something .... people's expectations, they are as
good as they are expected to be.

3 If you .... , you work at the necessary speed so that you do as
well as other people or get all your work done in the required time.

4 If you .... a problem or difficulty, you are faced with it and
have to deal with it.

2 Match the phrases on the left with those on the right.

1 His marks are fine
2 His situation was desperate,
3 If you're absent for two weeks,
4 The only question is this:
5 The child soon comes up against

A you're going to have to work very hard
   to catch up.
B but he faced up to it.
C can he live up to their expectations of
   him?
D and he doesn't seem to have any trouble
   keeping up.
E a whole system of prohibitions.

1	2	3	4	5

3 Choose the best alternative from the phrasal verbs
given to fill in the space provided.

1 Fortunately both surgeon and anaesthetist .... the high
standards of care expected of them.
came up against   lived up to   caught up

2 We may as well .... the fact that it isn't going to work.
face up to   live up to   come up against

3 Simon tried to .... the others.
catch up with   come up against   live up to

4 Everyone .... discrimination sooner or later.
lives up to   catches up   comes up against

5 Congratulations and .... the good work!
catch up with   face up to   keep up

4 Write the correct form of the appropriate phrasal
verb in the space provided.

1 Most leaders were obsessed with .... with the West.

2 If you .... any problems, give me a call.

3 She succeeded, to my mind, in .... her extraordinary
reputation.

4 The scale of change everyone needs to .... is that over the last
five years the Sotheby's Index has shown art prices rising by 150%.

5 It is important to .... a certain standard of dress and be
consistent.

5 Write a paragraph on the topic of your choice,
including at least one example of each of the phrasal
verbs you have just studied.

D Disrupting and Damaging

blow up break up hold up mess up mix up slip up

They now have enough nuclear weapons to blow themselves up many times over.

The Soviet Union has broken up.

The European Community threatened to hold up[1] the negotiations.

If she got caught with me now it would mess up[2] the rest of her life.

I have somehow mixed up two events.

We must have slipped up[3] somewhere.

◆ **LANGUAGE COMMENT**

1 **Delay** means almost the same as **hold up.**

2 This is an informal use. **Screw up** means almost the same as **mess up,** but is very informal.

3 This is an informal expression. There is also a noun:
   A similar slip-up occurred later in the week.

1 Match the sentences and phrases on the left with those on the right.

1 This is an update,
2 Well, gentlemen, any other business?
3 How can anyone do such a bad job?
4 He said he'd been held up.
5 One of the submarines blew up
6 She's slipped up in the calculations;

A She's really messed it up this time.
B He might be a minute or two late.
C If not, we'll break up the meeting and have a drink.
D I don't think it can be as much as that.
E don't mix it up with the other version.
F and sank.

1	2	3	4	5	6

2 Choose the best alternative from the phrasal verbs
given to fill in the space provided.

1 He tried to .... the Houses of Parliament.
slip up   blow up   hold up

2 That will .... the whole analysis.
blow up   slip up   mess up

3 The whole thing was .... about half an hour.
blown up   broken up   held up

4 His committee .... into rival groups.
blew up   held up   broke up

5 I got .... and forgot which interview I'd gone to first.
blown up   mixed up   slipped up

6 Someone's .... again, they've sent the wrong cassette.
slipped up   held up   broken up

3 Write the correct form of the appropriate phrasal
verb in the space provided.

1 If there's any delay, it'll .... the rest of our plans.

2 Headquarters has .... again: the letter wasn't sent.

3 The battleship Maine has been .... in Havana Harbour.

4 Their marriage is ....

5 People even .... us .... and greet us by each other's names.

6 The amount of animal research being carried out is probably
.... progress rather than increasing it.

4 Find the logical ending for each of the jokes beginning
on the left.

1 Did you hear about the stupid terrorist who tried to blow up a bus?

2 A man rushed into a bank and pointed his finger at the cashier. 'This is a mess-up!'

3 My boyfriend and I broke up. He wanted to get married,

A and I didn't want him to.
B He burnt his lips on the exhaust pipe.
C 'Don't you mean hold-up?' said the cashier. 'No, mess-up - I forgot my gun.'

1	2	3

E Completing and Finishing **Part 1**

**check up clear up cover up do up
drink up end up follow up**

The council had <u>checked up</u> on her and decided that she was unsuitable for employment.

Inspector Standish was trying to <u>clear up</u>[1] a tiresome problem.

I'm going back till this weather <u>clears up</u>.

He alleged that the President knew about Watergate and tried to <u>cover it up</u>[2].

I can't <u>do my top button up</u>[3].

<u>Drink up</u>. Here comes another bottle of wine.

If we go on in this way, we shall <u>end up</u>[4] with millions and millions of unemployed.

It's an idea which has been <u>followed up</u>[5] by the local council.

'It says he's an egotistical, shallow, insincere little bore and if he's not careful he could <u>end up</u> with his own chat show.'

◆ LANGUAGE COMMENT

1 **Sort out** means almost the same as **clear up**.

2 **Conceal** and **suppress** are more formal words for **cover up**.
There is also a noun:
He denied that he took any part in the <u>cover-up</u>.

3 **Fasten up** means almost the same as **do up**. **Belt up, button up, tie up** and **zip up** are all similar but are more specific.

4 **Finish up** and **wind up** mean almost the same as **end up**.

5 **Investigate** is a more formal word for **follow up**.

1 Match the phrases on the left with those on the right.

1 They think there is a security leak
2 I'm assuming that the misunderstanding
3 Look, it's cleared up now,
4 Sylvia ended up with no money, no husband
5 Drink your milk up
6 He started to do up his boots,
7 I'd like you to follow up this information
8 It has to be covered up:

A pulling fiercely at the laces.
B and then you can go out and play.
C and no house and a two-year-old child.
D if the public find out, we're finished.
E we received on scanners.
F will be cleared up soon.
G and are trying to check up.
H we could go for our walk.

1	2	3	4	5	6	7	8

2 Choose the best alternative from the phrasal verbs
   given to fill in the space provided.

1 Well, I'm glad we managed to .... that little problem.
   do up   clear up   drink up

2 He would undo a window cord, ... it .... again and walk back.
   check up   do up   end up

3 We .... taking a taxi there.
   followed up   ended up   did up

4 .... It's time to go.
   Drink up   End up   Do up

5 He had been aware that they would be .... on him.
   covering up   checking up   clearing up

6 It's an idea which has been .... by a group of researchers at
   Birmingham.
   followed up   done up   ended up

7 If the weather .... tomorrow, we'll go up into the mountains.
   follows up   clears up   covers up

8 She tried to .... for Willie.
   cover up   do up   end up

3 Write the correct form of the appropriate phrasal
   verb in the space provided.

1 I .... an advertisement for a second-hand Volkswagen.

2 Many of their friends .... in prison for terrorist activities.

3 He .... his shoelaces ....

4 The two of them .... a whole bottle of gin.

5 Let's hope the weather .... for Joanna's birthday party.

6 We have a lot of work to .... before the end of the year.

7 The police are .... on his story.

8 She hoped to .... anything unpleasant that might be said.

107

E Completing and Finishing Part 2

**give up   pull up   sum up
tidy up   use up   weigh up
wind up**

I'll never be able to give up smoking.

*The rain stopped as we pulled up
to the hotel.*

*I can't sum up his whole philosophy
in one sentence.*

*He went back to the studio and
tidied it up[1].*

He used up all the coins he had.

*Having weighed everything up[2],
he must have decided it was the
right thing to do.*

'*Your problem is exercise – I suggest you give up
jogging . . .*'

When my turn came to wind up the debate, I felt very nervous.

◆ **LANGUAGE COMMENT**

1 **Clear up** means almost the same as **tidy up**.
2 **Size up** means almost the same as **weigh up**.

1 Match the sentences and phrases on the left with those
on the right.

1 Aren't there any more cassettes?
2 Next time they thought of committing a
   crime
3 Sugar?
4 Ten to fifteen black-and-white police
   cars
5 To sum all this up,
6 They wound up the evening
7 Tidy everything up

A and put it away in my locker.
B had pulled up in front of the office.
C No, I gave it up during the war.
D No, we've used them all up.
E by watching a video of their last
   holiday.
F what we need is a reform of the grant-
   aid system.
G they would weigh it up and think, 'Well
   it just isn't worth it.'

1	2	3	4	5	6	7

2 Choose the best alternative from the phrasal verbs given to fill in the space provided.

1 Eva was .... after lunch.
tidying up   using up   weighing up

2 I don't have any intention of .... politics.
giving up   pulling up   summing up

3 You have to .... in your mind whether to pursue the matter or not.
give up   wind up   weigh up

4 At the end of the discussion, he .... , and added a few points.
weighed up   used up   summed up

5 He saw the two men in black .... behind his car and get out to watch the streets.
weigh up   pull up   tidy up

6 He .... his talk by showing us a model of the proposed extension.
used up   weighed up   wound up

7 She did .... a tremendous amount of energy.
pull up   use up   weigh up

3 Write the correct form of the appropriate phrasal verb in the space provided.

1 She never completely .... hope.

2 I am .... the pros and the cons.

3 Eventually, I signalled that it was time to .... the game.

4 If we go on spending like this, we'll .... all our money.

5 She was searching for the words that would .... it ....

6 A van approaches and has to ....

7 I started to .... the drawers.

109

4 Find the logical ending for each of the jokes beginning
on the left.

1 Why did your uncle give up being a taxi
   driver?

2 Did you hear the rumour about the
   watchmaker?

3 The way his horses ran could be
   summed up in a word.

4 What did one dragon say to the other
   dragon?

5 Why did the doctor tell you to give up
   golf? Are you sick?

A No, he saw my score card.

B I keep trying to give up smoking, but I
   can't.

C He's just wound up his business.

D He drove all his customers away.

E Last.

1	2	3	4	5

5 Write a paragraph on the topic of your choice,
including at least one example of each of the phrasal
verbs you have just studied.

F Happening and Creating

bring up   come up   come up with
make up   pick up   think up   turn up

I advised her to bring the matter up[1] at the next meeting.

I can't see you tonight. Something's come up[2].

The European Community commission came up with a compromise.

He was a good storyteller, and used to make up tales about animals.

Did you pick up any Turkish while you were in Turkey?

I may pick up a couple of useful ideas for my book.

I kept thinking up[3] ways I could murder him without getting caught.

Protein turns up in almost every food.

'If you ask me, he makes up half of his war stories.'

◆ **LANGUAGE COMMENT**

1 **Raise** means almost the same as **bring up**.

2 **Crop up** means almost the same as **come up**.

3 **Dream up** means almost the same as **think up**.

1 Write the correct phrasal verb to complete the following definitions.

1 If you .... a skill or habit, you learn it without making any effort.

2 When you .... a particular subject, you mention it or introduce it into a discussion or conversation.

3 If you .... a plan, idea, or solution, you think of it and suggest it.

4 If you .... a clever idea, you use your imagination or intelligence to create it.

5 If you .... something such as a story, you invent it, sometimes in order to deceive people.

2 Match the sentences and phrases on the left with those
on the right.

1 He was always boasting	A bargains in basement sales.
2 Yet no one had come up with	B he tended to become evasive.
3 If anything urgent comes up	C you can always get me on the phone.
4 Her mother had liked to pick up	D where did you pick it up.
5 The missing book turned up	E and making up stories about where he had been.
6 Whenever she brought up the topic of money,	F a system which was infallible.
7 I didn't know you could play the guitar,	G three weeks later in the stationery cupboard.
8 'Some suggestion.' Calderwood snorted.	H 'Did you think this up all by yourself?'

1	2	3	4	5	6	7	8

3 Choose the best alternative from the phrasal verbs
given to fill in the space provided.

1 Sometimes a case of stealing is .... at the General School
Meeting.
thought up   come up with   brought up

2 Something pretty urgent seems to have .... , and she'd like you
to ring her up this afternoon.
brought up   picked up   come up

3 She told herself, 'Don't be stupid; you're .... things ....'
making up   bringing up   coming up

4 Lo had had ample time to .... the rudiments of driving.
make up   pick up   bring up

5 ...some kind of food poisoning that they .... at dinner.
turned up   picked up   brought up

6 It didn't take her long to .... a very convincing example.
turn up   come up with   pick up

7 You must be willing to take a job as soon as one ....
comes up with   makes up   turns up

8 He informed me of a new financial agreement he had ....
thought up   come up   brought up

4 Write the correct form of the appropriate phrasal
verb in the space provided.

1 A rather delicate assignment has ....

2 Babies can easily .... thrush, a mild fungus infection.

3 Whoever .... this idea needs his head examined.

4 The kids .... it .... really fast but lose it just as quickly.

5 You don't need to jump on a child for .... stories occasionally,
or make him feel guilty.

6 I am sorry to .... the subject of politics yet again.

7 The odds against such a ratio .... by chance must be
astronomical.

8 I hope to .... some of the answers.

5 Write a paragraph on the topic of your choice,
including at least one example of each of the phrasal
verbs you have just studied.

G Collecting and Being together

**look up make up pick up put up
take up on**

Look me up when you're next in the area.

*Women now make up two-fifths of the British
labour force.*

*Can you pick up the kids from school tonight?
I've got a meeting.*

The Murrays had put him up for the night.

*That's very kind of you, Mr Zapp, I'll take you up on
that generous invitation.*

1 Write the correct phrasal verb to complete the
following definitions.

1 If you .... someone .... , you visit the person after not having seen
them for a long time.

2 If you .... someone .... an offer they have made, you accept their
offer.

3 If someone .... you .... , you stay with them for one or more
nights.

4 The people or things that .... something form that thing.

5 If you are driving a vehicle and you .... someone or something .... ,
you stop the vehicle so that you can take them somewhere.

2 Match the sentences and phrases on the left with those
on the right.

1 She paused a while,
2 She was put up
3 When you're in Switzerland you must
   look up my niece Patricia.
4 I picked up a hitchhiker
5 Nearly half the Congress

A is made up of lawyers.
B I'll send you her address.
C in case he might care to take her up on
   her offer.
D at the Grand Hotel.
E on the way back from Zurich.

1	2	3	4	5

3 Choose the best alternative from the phrasal verbs
given to fill in the space provided.

1 Young people from eighteen to thirty .... a third of the Civil
Defence force.
put up look up make up

2 We can't .... him .... here.
put up take up on make up

3 But this suggestion is absurd, and no one .... him .... it.
looked up picked up took up on

4 You can .... people, you know, that you haven't seen for a long
time.
look up pick up make up

5 Will anyone be able to .... me .... from the station?
put up pick up look up

4 Write the correct form of the appropriate phrasal
verb in the space provided.

1 The committee, ... equally of men and women, sat around a
long table.

2 I hope he doesn't .... you .... your offer to stay with us until he
finds a flat.

3 He told me to .... him .... if I was ever in the area.

4 You don't have to stay in a hotel, we can .... you ....

5 Don't forget to .... the clothes .... from the dry cleaner's.

5 Write a paragraph on the topic of your choice,
including at least one example of each of the phrasal
verbs you have just studied.

115

H Other meanings

**look up   make up for   put up with
take up   turn up**

*He consulted his dictionary to
look up the meaning of the word
'apotheosis'.*

*She asked me questions about my
interest in mathematics, as if to
make up for excluding me from the
conversation.*

*I'm prepared to put up with[1] it
for the time being.*

She decided to take up[2] medicine as a career.

If it's a boring game the crowds won't turn up[3] next time.

*'I do love you. But, to be perfectly
honest, I would have loved any
lovebird who happened
to turn up.'*

◆ **LANGUAGE COMMENT**

1 **Endure** is a more formal word for **put up with**.

2 **Go in for** means almost the same as **take up**.

3 **Show up** means almost the same as **turn up**.

1 **Write the correct phrasal verb to complete the
following definitions.**

1 To .... something that is damaged, lost, or missing means to
replace it or compensate for it.

2 If you .... a piece of information in a book, or on a timetable or
map, you look there to find the information.

3 If you .... an activity or job, you start doing it.

4 If someone .... , they arrive somewhere.

5 If you .... something or someone, you tolerate or accept them,
even though you find it difficult or unpleasant.

2 Match the phrases on the left with those on the right.

1 Religion disciplined us and gave us the strength
2 And why, at the age of thirty,
3 Lally said it would help me with my geography
4 But most of those who had attended in the morning
5 Massive reductions in other areas would be required

A he took up architecture, is not clear.
B if I went and looked it up on a map.
C to put up with things.
D turned up again for the afternoon session.
E to make up for the expected shortfall in revenues.

1	2	3	4	5

3 Write the correct form of the appropriate phrasal verb in the space provided.

1 You have to .... these inconveniences as best you can.

2 Why don't you .... the address in the directory?

3 At Summerhill, three boys, inspired by jazz bands, ... musical instruments.

4 I'm not late, I haven't failed to .... , I'm here and I'm hungry.

5 McEnroe is asking his talent alone to .... a shortage of match practice.

BadJokes

4 Find the logical ending for each of the jokes beginning on the left.

1 What he lacks in intelligence,
2 Did you hear about the secretary who was a miracle?
3 My son has taken up meditation -
4 Do you think my son should take up the piano as a career?

A No, I think he should put down the lid as a favour.
B at least it's better than sitting doing nothing.
C It was a miracle if she turned up to work on time.
D he makes up for in stupidity.

1	2	3	4

UP **Revision exercises**

1 Choose the best alternative from the phrasal verbs given to fill in the space provided.

1 My marriage .... in 1967, leaving me with three small children.
   went up   broke up   warmed up   stirred up

2 In Africa and the Indian subcontinent women .... about a third of the workforce.
   cheer up   make up   use up   push up

3 But I thought he'd asked Janet to .... on that.
   mix up   blow up   think up   follow up

4 I wish that people would .... after themselves.
   tidy up   take up   weigh up   dress up

5 If she wishes to work rather than to stay at home and .... her children, she should be entirely free to do so.
   grow up   push up   warm up   bring up

6 I went to .... the matter .... with him.
   use up   clear up   catch up   back up

7 There are hundreds of huge old houses in the south east that people are

   .... to sell at a profit.
   building up   coming up against   holding up   doing up

8 It was South Africa's isolation that was forcing President de Klerk to

   .... the need for changes.
   face up to   fix up   turn up   put up

9 He never reached the mountain. After the third day he .... , exhausted.
   brushed up   gave up   grew up   used up

10 'Girls,' he said, 'a really bad thing has .... Bad for me, I mean, not for you. Fine for you.
   brought up   slipped up   come up   picked up

11 A pharmaceutical researcher told me of being .... for three or four hours by border guards.
   turned up   held up   speeded up   covered up

12 He .... this .... with a few horrifying anecdotes.
   backed up   came up   made up for   spoke up

13 I can't .... it .... , there must be something caught in the zip.
   blow up   do up   drink up   mix up

14 The newspaper correctly reported that the government had .... a committee.
    set up   drawn up   summed up   checked up

15 The visitors .... any amount of boredom.
    come up with   put up with   bring up   look up

16 If you .... it .... again, you'll be looking for a new job.
    speak up   end up   slip up   mess up

17 Japan successfully .... a modern capitalist society.
    did up   built up   turned up   put up

18 .... the address of the nearest children's clinic.
    Use up   Cheer up   Look up   Sum up

19 By the time we .... the conversation, I knew that I would not be going to Geneva.
    softened up   wound up   came up against   kept up

20 Leaders had not .... their duties, failed to curb extremists and had inflamed the situation.
    come up against   looked up   held up   lived up to

21 Trade should .... just before Christmas and drop off in February.
    fix up   pick up   take up on   draw up

22 It took me a year to .... for a new coat.
    pick up   save up   take up   build up

23 Children .... with or without parental guidance.
    grow up   weigh up   bring up   go up

24 He was in New York, ... on his image as an expert in foreign affairs.
    softening up   cheering up   brushing up   turning up

25 .... a list of all the problems we've been having with the new computers.
    Set up   Draw up   Weigh up   Wind up

26 A Danish journalist .... to interview the old guy.
    turned up   made up   took up   thought up

27 You have to .... the options very carefully before taking a decision.
    end up   weigh up   stir up   mix up

28 They had to conform to a way of life to .... appearances.
    catch up   turn up   cheer up   keep up

2 Complete the phrasal verbs in the six groups
illustrated below. Check your answers on page 95.

b......k up
b.........g up
br......h up
b......ld up
ch......... up
d... up
dr......... up
g... up

g......w up
p......k up
p......h up
s...e up
sp......k up
s.........d up
s......r up

A Increasing and Improving

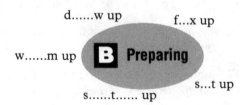

d......w up

f...x up

w......m up

B Preparing

s...t up

s......t...... up

C Approaching

c......ch up
c......... up ag.........st
f......e up t...
k......p up
l......... up t...

D Disrupting and Damaging

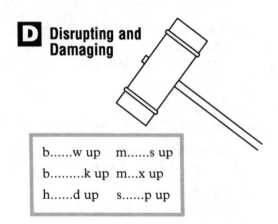

b......w up   m......s up
b.........k up   m...x up
h......d up   s......p up

E Completing and Finishing

cl......... up
c...u...... up
f...ll...... up
g......e up

p......l up
s...m up
w......gh up
w......d up

STOP

ch......... up
t......y up
u...... up

d... up
dr......... up
e...d up

F Happening and Creating

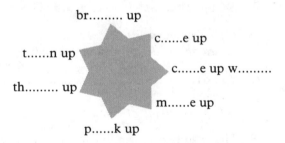

br......... up

c......e up

t......n up

c......e up w.........

th......... up

m......e up

p......k up

OTHER PARTICLES

Below are seven more particles, each with one group of phrasal verbs. In all there are 30 phrasal verbs to practise.

You can write other phrasal verbs with the same meaning in the space provided. Use a dictionary if necessary.

AHEAD Making progress or Thinking about the future

get ahead
go ahead
lie ahead
plan ahead

....

....

....

BY Being prepared, Surviving, and Visiting

drop by
get by
put by
stand by

....

....

....

TOGETHER Being in groups and organizing things

get together
piece together
pull together
put together

....

....

....

APART Undoing or Collapsing

fall apart
take apart (two meanings)
tear apart

....

....

FORWARD Looking to the future and Presenting something

bring forward
go forward
look forward to
put forward

....

....

....

....

....

AROUND/ROUND/ABOUT

Changing opinions, Avoiding, and Being inactive

bring about
bring around/round
get around/round
get around/round to
stick around

....

....

....

THROUGH Completing and Being thorough

fall through
go through with
pull through
put through
think through

....

....

....

....

AHEAD Making progress or Thinking about the future

get ahead   go ahead   lie ahead   plan ahead

The only way to get ahead[1] is to move to another company.

The case will be discussed and he will be told whether or not he can go ahead[2].

Many seemingly insurmountable obstacles lay ahead.

They advised him to plan ahead[3] for an election.

◆ LANGUAGE COMMENT

1 **Get on** means almost the same as **get ahead**.

2 **Proceed** is a more formal word for **go ahead**.
   There is also a noun:
   You have the go-ahead from the Prime Minister.
   There is a related adjective:
   ...its go-ahead young secretary.
   Forge ahead, plough ahead, press ahead and **push ahead** all
   have similar meanings.

3 **Think ahead** means almost the same as **plan ahead**.

1 Write the correct phrasal verb to complete the
following definitions.

1 If you .... , you make arrangements in advance for some thing.

2 If you .... , you are successful in your career.

3 If an event or situation .... , it is likely to happen in the future.

4 When someone .... with something which they planned,
promised, or asked permission to do, they begin to do it.

2 Match the phrases on the left with those on the right.

1 The ballot
2 The task that lies ahead
3 Few individuals or families
4 He's really got ahead incredibly quickly

A looks positively frightening.
B will go ahead immediately.
C for someone who only joined the firm
    three years ago.
D plan ahead systematically.

1	2	3	4

3 Choose the best alternative from the phrasal verbs given to fill in the space provided.

1 What .... of them?
planned ahead   lay ahead   went ahead

2 I admire people who ....
lay ahead   go ahead   plan ahead

3 The May day marches could ....
go ahead   plan ahead   lay ahead

4 You've really got to be sharp to ....
lay ahead   get ahead   plan ahead

4 Write the correct form of the appropriate phrasal verb in the space provided.

1 If you want to .... in this world, you've got to work, work, work.

2 To be successful in business you have to .... months or years ....

3 Harder decisions ....

4 They are .... with the missile.

5 Write a paragraph on the topic of your choice, including at least one example of each of the phrasal verbs you have just studied.

APART Undoing and Collapsing

fall apart take apart tear apart

The treaty is falling apart[1] before it has even come into effect.

Their tasks include taking apart[2] and reassembling large bits of furniture.

He had read the material and was prepared to take apart[3] the statement that rhetoric is an art.

He was fighting against the 'anarchy' which he insisted was tearing the Church apart.

◆ **LANGUAGE COMMENT**

1 **Collapse** means almost the same as **fall apart**.

2 **Dismantle** is a more formal word for **take apart**; **put together** means the opposite.

3 **Pull apart** and **tear apart** mean almost the same as **take apart**.

1 Write the correct phrasal verb to complete the following definitions.

1 If something .... a person, organization, or country .... , it causes them to experience great conflicts or disturbances.

2 If you .... something such as an argument, you analyse it carefully in order to show what its weaknesses are.

3 If an organization, system or relationship .... , it no longer works effectively and eventually fails or ends completely.

4 If you .... something .... , you separate it into the different parts that it is made from.

2 Match the phrases on the left with those on the right.

1 They have lived through so much together;

2 Most of these machines have to be taken apart

3 The conference fell apart

4 She simply took apart my chapter

A to be cleaned.

B what could possibly tear them apart?

C with the same techniques that I had used to take apart her essay.

D when the President refused to participate.

1	2	3	4

3 Choose the best alternative from the phrasal verbs
given to fill in the space provided.

1   The essay had not been a particularly great success and I'd .... it
    .... somewhat.
    fallen apart   torn apart   taken apart

2   The nation is .... at the seams.
    falling apart   tearing apart   taking apart

3   She is .... by conflicting pressures.
    taken apart   torn apart   fallen apart

4   We encouraged them to explore, invent, ... things .... , and put
    them together.
    tear apart   fall apart   take apart

4 Write the correct form of the appropriate phrasal
verb in the space provided.

1   I'll have to .... the bike ....

2   These were the agonies which were .... him ....

3   I have never enjoyed watching anyone .... a book .... in public,
    but this time it was justified.

4   Their marriage began to ....

5 Write a paragraph on the topic of your choice,
including at least one example of each of the phrasal
verbs you have just studied.

AROUND/ROUND/ABOUT Changing opinions, Avoiding, and Being inactive

bring about   bring around/round   get around/round get around/round to   stick around

The Administration helped bring about a peaceful settlement.
We tried to bring him round¹ to our point of view.
An impasse has developed and I don't know how to get around² it.
I didn't get round to³ taking the examination.
Mike wanted me to stick around⁴ for a couple of days.

◆ LANGUAGE COMMENT

1 **Bring around** means the same as **bring round; come round** and **win over** mean almost the same.

2 **Get round** means the same as **get around**.

3 **Get round to** means the same as **get around to**.

4 **Hang around** and **stay around** mean almost the same as **stick around**.

1 Write the correct phrasal verb to complete the following definitions.

1 To .... something .... means to cause it to happen.

2 If you .... or .... a difficulty or restriction, you find a way of avoiding it or of escaping its effects.

3 If you ...., you stay where you are, often because you are waiting for something.

4 If you .... or .... doing something, you do it after a long delay because you were previously too busy or reluctant to do it.

5 If someone disagrees with you and you .... them .... , you cause them to change their opinion and agree with you.

2 Match the sentences and phrases on the left with those on the right.

1 I only got around to
2 I'll stick around
3 It is up to you to outwit them
4 To get round the law
5 But why was all this happening?

A and bring them round to your side.
B their plays were staged on private property.
C What had brought it about?
D and keep an eye on the food.
E doing the other things a few days ago.

1	2	3	4	5

126

3 Choose the best alternative from the phrasal verbs given to fill in the space provided.

1 It took her two years to .... buying a car.
   get around to   bring about   bring round

2 A good lawyer should be able to find a way to .... that clause.
   get around to   bring about   get round

3 Jackson tried to .... him .... to our way of thinking.
   bring about   stick around   bring round

4 ...the smog .... by car exhausts.
   got around to   brought about   stuck around

5 Maybe I'll just .... here for a while.
   stick around   get round   bring round

4 Write the correct form of the appropriate phrasal verb in the space provided.

1 There's nothing else to .... for.

2 Naturally, one wonders what may have taken place to .... the separation
   ....

3 To help .... this problem, some tanks are now equipped with radar.

4 David's father didn't want to let him use the car, but in the end David ....
   him ....

5 It was only on the following day that the Police finally ....
   interviewing Meehan.

5 Write a paragraph on the topic of your choice, including at least one example of each of the phrasal verbs you have just studied.

BY Being prepared, Surviving, and Visiting

drop by get by put by stand by

If there's anything you want to see, just drop by[1].

You can get by in any English conversation with a very limited vocabulary.

You should start putting something by[2] for when the chidren are older.

Government engineers were standing by[3] to provide emergency repairs in the event of a breakdown.

◆ **LANGUAGE COMMENT**

1 **Drop in, drop round, come by, come round** and **stop by** mean almost the same as **drop by.**

2 **Put aside** and **set aside** mean almost the same as **put by.**

3 There is also a noun:
It was one of three Boeings put on standby for the trip.

1 **Write the correct phrasal verb to complete the following definitions.**

1 If you .... in a difficult situation, you manage to cope with it.

2 To .... means to visit someone informally without having arranged the visit.

3 If you .... , you are ready to provide help or take action if it becomes necessary.

4 If you .... a sum of money or a supply of something, you save it so that you can use it later.

2 **Match the phrases on the left with those on the right.**

1 Stand by with lots of water
2 It's always a good idea
3 It's possible to get by
4 Martin dropped by this afternoon

A to have something put by.
B and sends you his regards.
C in case a fire breaks out.
D in a job interview by just talking about your interests.

1	2	3	4

3 Choose the best alternative from the phrasal verbs given to fill in the space provided.

1 Arthur Coggs had prudently .... it .... for future use.
stood by put by dropped by

2 She .... in French all right, but she needs to improve her German.
gets by stands by puts by

3 .... whenever you want.
Stand by Drop by Get by

4 The Government ordered the troops to ....
get by drop by stand by

4 Write the correct form of the appropriate phrasal verb in the space provided.

1 Although the budget's been cut for the coming year, we should just

....

2 I'll be .... in case of trouble, so don't worry.

3 You'll never guess who .... at the office this morning.

4 With what he'd .... , he could live in luxury for the rest of his life.

5 Write a paragraph on the topic of your choice, including at least one example of each of the phrasal verbs you have just studied.

FORWARD Looking to the future and Presenting something

bring forward   go forward   look forward to   put forward

Ask him to <u>bring the meeting forward</u>[1] to eight o'clock.

Preparations were <u>going forward</u> for the annual Caxley Musical Festival.

I'm quite <u>looking forward to</u> seeing Rick again.

The TUC <u>put forward</u>[2] a plan for national recovery.

◆ LANGUAGE COMMENT

1 **Put forward** means almost the same as **bring forward**; **put back** means the opposite.

2 **Propose** and **set out** mean almost the same as **put forward**.

1 **Write the correct phrasal verb to complete the following definitions.**

1   If you .... an idea or proposal, you state it or publish it so that people can consider it and discuss it.

2   If you .... something that is going to happen, you want it to happen because you expect to enjoy it.

3   If you .... a meeting or an event, you arrange for it to be at an earlier time or date than was planned.

4   If something .... , it makes progress and begins to happen.

2 **Match the phrases on the left with those on the right.**

1   I did not look forward with any confidence
2   Lipset does not put the proposition forward
3   The match would have
4   If our present plans go forward

A   to my meeting with the manager.
B   we shall bring in an assistant for you.
C   as a universal truth.
D   to be brought forward.

1	2	3	4

3 Choose the best alternative from the phrasal verbs
given to fill in the space provided.

1   They rejected every proposal ....
    gone forward   looked forward to   put forward

2   We have to .... , push ahead, if not we'll stagnate.
    go forward   look forward to   bring forward

3   I .... seeing you in Washington.
    go forward   put forward   look forward to

4   We would need the delivery date .... by one month.
    brought forward   gone forward   looked forward to

4 Write the correct form of the appropriate phrasal
verb in the space provided.

1   Let's hope everything .... as planned.

2   The meeting has been .... to Tuesday.

3   The idea was first .... by J.Good.

4   I .... leaving school next summer.

5 Write a paragraph on the topic of your choice,
including at least one example of each of the phrasal
verbs you have just studied.

THROUGH   Completing and Being thorough

fall through   go through with   pull through   put through   think through

But the scheme <u>fell through</u>, despite all my careful instructions.

The government was determined to <u>go through with</u> that legislation.

The doctors managed to <u>pull her through</u> a long and difficult illness.

They <u>put through</u> the first nuclear arms agreements.

I haven't really <u>thought the whole business through</u> in my own mind.

'I see the Hitachi deal <u>fell through</u>.'

1 Write the correct phrasal verb to complete the following definitions.

1   If people in authority

.... a proposal
or plan, they formally agree to it.

2   If you .... a situation .... , you consider it thoroughly, together with all its possible effects or consequences.

3   If an arrangement or plan .... , something goes wrong with it before it can be completed and it has to be abandoned.

4   If you .... a decision or an action, you continue to do what is necessary in order to achieve it or complete it.

5   When someone who is very ill .... , they recover.

2 Match the sentences and phrases on the left with those on the right.

1   He was planning to put through his deal,

2   I've been thinking it all through

3   She's down at the hospital with him.

4   I'm still pregnant.

5   When my project to film the North Wall of the Eiger fell through,

A   and I do just want to see for myself.

B   I didn't go through with the abortion.

C   I thought up a more modest scheme.

D   despite official US disapproval.

E   The doctors said he'll pull through.

1	2	3	4	5

3 Choose the best alternative from the phrasal verbs given to fill in the space provided.

1 The present Government have decided to .... Part One of the Labour Government's Bill for a Health Service in industry.
pull through   put through   think through

2 I realised, with increasing force, that I could not .... another major expedition the following spring.
put through   go through with   pull through

3 He's in very bad shape. He'll .... but he needs all kinds of attention.
pull through   go through   put through

4 He was determined to .... the difficulty rather than remain baffled.
fall through   put through   think through

5 The sale of your house has .... at the last minute.
pulled through   thought through   fallen through

4 Write the correct form of the appropriate phrasal verb in the space provided.

1 I had a rough old time from then on, I can tell you! But I .... I've got to eighty-five in spite of it all.

2 I cannot explain this easily. I was determined to .... it, and yet I was not serious about it.

3 I didn't manage to let my flat after all, it ....

4 It really needs to be .... much more than this, before we proceed.

5 They had at last succeeded in .... a meaningful reform ....

5 Write a paragraph on the topic of your choice, including at least one example of each of the phrasal verbs you have just studied.

TOGETHER Being in groups and Organizing things

get together   piece together   pull together   put together

Do you think we could get together[1] at Christmas?

She had not yet been able to piece together[2] exactly what happened.

That's quite enough of that. Pull yourself together now and stop this at once.

The shipyards possess years of expertise in putting together[3] such big metal structures.

◆ **LANGUAGE COMMENT**

1 There is also a noun:
We're having a little get-together to celebrate Helen's promotion.

2 **Work out** means almost the same as **piece together**; **deduce** is a more formal word.

3 **Assemble** is a more formal word for **put together**; **take apart** means the opposite.

1 Write the correct phrasal verb to complete the following definitions.

1 If you .... the truth about something, you gradually discover it.

2 If you .... an object or its parts, you join its parts to each other so that it can be used.

3 When you .... yourself .... , you control your feelings and behave calmly after you have been upset or angry.

4 When people .... , they meet in order to discuss something or to spend time together.

2 Match the phrases on the left with those on the right.

1 Pulling herself together,
2 Workers and supervisors
3 The agency has put together
4 I found out the truth

A by piecing together hints and rumours that I heard at school.
B get together to discuss their grievances.
C Mrs Oliver managed to fight back her annoyance.
D the biggest ever campaign for a new car.

1	2	3	4

3 Choose the best alternative from the phrasal verbs
given to fill in the space provided.

1 It says here that a child of 5 can .... it ....
put together   pull together   get together

2 As the questioning continued he began to .... it ....
pull together   piece together   get together

3 .... yourself .... ; don't let them see you like this.
Piece together   Pull together   Put together

4 We really should .... as soon as possible to discuss the strategy
for next year.
get together   pull together   piece together

4 Write the correct form of the appropriate phrasal
verb in the space provided.

1 Can you .... with Henry to arrange the wedding reception?

2 He had taken some minutes alone in his room to .... himself ....

3 Grease the valve thoroughly and .... the parts .... again.

4 Using manuscript sources, it has been possible to .... the whole story
....

5 Write a paragraph on the topic of your choice,
including at least one example of each of the phrasal
verbs you have just studied.

ANSWER KEY

AWAY

A Withdrawing and Separating

1 1E 2F 3B 4A 5D 6C
2 1 run away
  2 keep away
  3 broke away
  4 took away
  5 get away
3 1 keep away
  2 give away
  3 ran away
  4 broke away
  5 get away
  6 taken away
4 1E 2A 3B 4C 5D

B Disappearing and Making things disappear

1 1 fades away
  2 throw away
  3 explain away
  4 do away with
2 1D 2E 3C 4B 5A
3 1 done away with
  2 passed away
  3 throw away
  4 fade away
  5 explain away
4 1 explained away
  2 Throw away
  3 passed away
  4 do away with
  5 faded away
5 1C 2A 3B

C Other meanings

1 1 hide away
  2 work away
  3 put away
  4 write away
  5 get away with
2 1B 2E 3A 4C 5D
3 1 worked away
  2 get away with
  3 put away
  4 hide away
  5 Write away

Revision exercises

1 1 throw away
  2 explain away
  3 working away
  4 get away
  5 do away with
  6 get away with
  7 broken away
  8 give away

BACK

A Returning or Repeating something

1 1G 2E 3B 4F 5D 6A 7C 8H
2 1 get back
  2 gave back
  3 go back over
  4 take back
  5 bounce back
  6 go back on
  7 call back
3 1 take back, give back
  2 get back
  3 go back on
  4 call back
  5 gave back
  6 fall back on

B Controlling or Suppressing

1 1C 2D 3B 4A
2 1 cut back
  2 hold back
  3 set back
  4 fighting back
3 1 set back
  2 hold back
  3 cut back
  4 fight back

Revision exercises

1 1 fall back on
  2 call back
  3 cut back
  4 went back over
  5 give back
  6 going back on
  7 get back
2 1A 2B 3A 4B

DOWN

A Decreasing and Reducing Part 1

1 1 comes down to
  2 dies down
  3 cut down
  4 comes down
2 1D 2F 3C 4A 5B 6E
3 1 comes down to
  2 cut down
  3 calming down
  4 die down
  5 brought down
  6 come down
4 1 come down
  2 bring down
  3 calmed down
  4 died down
  5 cut down
  6 comes down to

A Decreasing and Reducing Part 2

1 1 narrow down
  2 play down
  3 run down
  4 keep down
2 1B 2F 3C 4A 5E 6D
3 1 slow down
  2 run down
  3 narrow down
  4 played down
  5 scaled down
  6 keeps down
4 1 narrowed down, had narrowed down
  2 run down
  3 scale down
  4 slowed down, had slowed down
  5 keep down
  6 play down

B Defeating and Suppressing

1 1 clamp down
  2 wear down
  3 back down
2 1D 2E 3C 4G 5A 6F 7B

3 1 wearing down
  2 backed down
  3 knocked down
  4 clamped down
  5 pulled down
  6 put down
  7 brought down
4 1 puts down
  2 pull down, knock down
  3 backed down
  4 knocked down
  5 wearing down
  6 bring down
  7 clamped down

C Completing or Failing

1 1F 2C 3E 4A 5B 6D
2 1 turn down
  2 closing down
  3 broke down
  4 stand down
  5 let down
  6 settle down
3 1 let down
  2 turned down
  3 breaks down
  4 settle down
  5 closed down
  6 stand down

D Writing and Recording

1 1 put down
  2 take down
  3 put down to
  4 goes down as
  5 lay down
2 1C 2B 3D 4E 5A
3 1 put down
  2 put down to
  3 take down
  4 laid down
  5 go down as
4 1 taking down
  2 go down ... as
  3 put down
  4 laid down
  5 put down to

E Other meanings

1 1 talks down to
  2 live down
  3 pin down
  4 get down to
2 1D 2C 3B 4A

3 1 got down to
2 live down
3 talks down to
4 pin down

Revision exercises

1 1 play down
2 turn down
3 got down to
4 knocking down
5 lets down
6 bring down
7 clamp down
8 take down
9 died down
10 go down ... as
11 stand down
12 pin down
13 keep down
14 cut down
15 broken down
16 putting down

IN

A Inserting and Absorbing

1 1C 2D 3A 4B
2 1 plug in
2 put in
3 sink in
4 take in
3 1 plug in
2 took in
3 put in
4 sunk in

B Including

1 1 take in
2 throw in
3 fit in
4 fits in with
2 1B 2D 3C 4A
3 1 threw in
2 took in
3 fit in
4 fit in with
4 1 fit in
2 threw in
3 fit in ... with
4 take in

C Being involved and active

1 1D 2E 3F 4A 5G 6B 7C

2 1 gone in for
2 join in
3 called in
4 filled in
5 settled in
6 come in
7 putting in
3 1 fill in
2 called in
3 putting in
4 went in for
5 come in
6 settling in
7 joined in

D Beginning

1 1B 2D 3A 4C
2 1 phasing in
2 come in
3 set in
4 brought in
3 1 came in
2 bring in
3 phased in
4 set in

E Other meanings

1 1 give in
2 stay in
3 fill in
4 fill in
5 comes in for
2 1A 2D 3E 4B 5C
3 1 staying in
2 filling in
3 Fill in
4 give in
5 came in for

Revision exercise

1 1 fit in
2 fit in with
3 throw in
4 come in
5 put in
6 settling in
7 phase in
8 fill in
9 sets in
10 brought in
11 gave in
12 taking in
13 filling in
14 Go in for

ON

A Continuing

1 1 go on
2 rambles on
3 drags on
4 get on
5 keep on
2 1D 2B 3E 4G 5F 6A 7C
3 1 pass on
2 stay on
3 kept on
4 go on
5 rambling on
6 get on
7 dragged on
4 1 stay on
2 get on, go on
3 passed on
4 dragged on, gone on
5 got on, went on
6 ramble on
7 keep on

B Progressing

1 1 urge on
2 getting on
3 move on
4 coming on
2 1B 2D 3A 4C
3 1 getting on
2 urged on
3 move on
4 coming on
4 1 getting on
2 moved on
3 urge on
4 coming on

C Beginning

1 1 coming on
2 catches on
3 move on to
4 brings on
2 1C 2A 3D 4B
3 1 brought on
2 coming on
3 moved on to
4 catch on
4 1 move on to
2 coming on
3 brought on
4 catch on

D Other meanings

1 1 going on
2 go on
3 look on
4 take on
5 get on
6 lay on
2 1D 2F 3E 4A 5B 6C
3 1 go on
2 laid on
3 taken on
4 going on
5 got on
6 look on

Revision exercises

1 1C/D 2D/C 3A 4F 5B 6G 7E
2 1 getting on
2 takes on
3 go on
4 going on
5 get on
6 bring on
7 getting on
8 coming on
9 move on to
10 stayed on

OFF

A Leaving and Beginning

1 1 sparks off
2 see off
3 kick off
4 set off
2 1D 2E 3A 4F 5B 6C
3 1 sparked off
2 kick off
3 seeing off
4 drop off
5 set off
6 taken off
4 1 take off
2 see off
3 drop off
4 setting off
5 sparked off
6 kicked off

B Rejecting and Preventing

1 1 write off
2 put off
3 hold off
4 laid off
2 1E 2B 3D 4C 5A

3 1 hold off
2 lay off
3 put off
4 write off
5 keep off
4 1 putting off
2 keep off
3 hold off
4 laid off
5 written off

C Stopping and Cancelling

1 1C 2D 3A 4B
2 1 take off
2 broke off
3 let off
4 called off
3 1 called off
2 broke off
3 take off
4 let off

D Decreasing

1 1D 2E 3C 4A 5B
2 1 wear off
2 level off
3 work off
4 cooling off
5 fall off
3 1 work off
2 fall off
3 cooled off
4 level off
5 wore off

E Finishing and Completing

1 1D 2C 3A 4B
2 1 finishing off
2 pull off
3 went off
4 pay off
3 1 finish off
2 pull off
3 went off
4 pay off

F Other meanings

1 1 rips off
2 show off
3 goes off
4 goes off; goes off
5 tell off
2 1B 2C 3D 4E 5A

3 1 gone off
2 rip off
3 told off
4 going off
5 showing off

Revision exercise

1 1 pull off
2 spark off
3 call off
4 written off
5 goes off
6 lay off
7 set off
8 wear off
9 show off
10 laid off
11 went off
12 cool off
13 take off
14 broke off
15 told off

OUT

A Leaving and Beginning

1 1E 2C 3D 4A 5B
2 1 broke out
2 set out
3 gone out
4 checked out
5 taking out
3 1 break out
2 go out
3 took out, had taken out
4 set out
5 checking out
4 1C 2B 3A 4D 5E

B Removing and Excluding Part 1

1 1 cancels out; cancel out
2 keep out
3 get out of
2 1F 2C 3E 4B 5A 6D
3 1 cross out
2 keep out
3 cancel out
4 get out of
5 clean out
6 knocked out
4 1 clean out
2 get out of
3 crossed out
4 cancelled out
5 knocked out
6 keep out

B Removing and Excluding Part 2

1 1C 2D 3E 4A 5B 6F
2 1 talk ... out of
2 thrown out
3 opted out
4 ruled out
5 leave out
6 pull out
3 1 rule out
2 pulled out
3 opt out
4 throw out
5 talk ... out of
6 left out
4 1B 2C 3D 4A

C Searching and Finding

1 1 sound out
2 turns out
3 work out
4 make out
5 check out
2 1C 2F 3E 4B 5D 6A 7G
3 1 check out
2 trying out
3 found out
4 work out
5 make out
6 sounded out
7 turn out
4 1 sounded out
2 checking out
3 turned out
4 try out
5 find out, work out
6 work out
7 make out
5 1E 2C 3F 4B 5A 6D

D Producing and Creating

1 1 set out
2 speak out
3 put out
4 spell out
5 comes out
2 1C 2B 3E 4A 5D
3 1 spoke out
2 come out
3 spelled out
4 put out
5 set out

4 1 set out
2 put out
3 came out
4 speak out
5 spell out

E Supporting and Helping

1 1 look out
2 help out
3 bears out
4 point out
2 1D 2C 3B 4E 5A
3 1 pointed out
2 borne out
3 Look out
4 helped out
5 give out
4 1 pointed out
2 Look out
3 gave out
4 helped out
5 bear out

F Ending or Disappearing

1 1C 2D 3A 4E 5B
2 1 sold out
2 wearing out
3 ran out
4 wiped out
5 phase out
3 1 phased out
2 wipe out
3 run out, sold out
4 run out
5 wore out

G Other meanings

1 1 take out on
2 stands out
3 fall out
4 sort out
5 carry out
2 1 fell out
2 took ... out on
3 carried out
4 sorting out
5 stands out

Revision exercises

1
1 sort out
2 came out
3 fell out
4 broken out
5 rule out
6 spelled out
7 turn out
8 spoke out
9 cleaning out
10 carried out
11 set out
12 opting out
13 pointed out
14 throw out
15 running out
16 get out of
17 talked ... out of
18 take out
19 leave out
20 find out
21 borne out
22 work out

OVER

A Considering and Communicating

1
1 put over
2 talk over
3 look over
4 think over
2 1B 2D 3C 4A
3
1 looking over
2 talk over
3 Think over
4 put over
4
1 put over
2 talk over
3 look over
4 think over

B Changing and Transferring

1
1 hand over
2 take over
3 win over
4 change over
5 take over
2 1D 2A 3B 4C 5E
3
1 took over
2 win over
3 take over
4 changed over
5 hand over

4
1 taken over
2 changing over
3 handed over
4 winning over
5 take over

C Other meanings

1
1 passed over
2 runs over
3 get ... over with
4 smooth over
2 1D 2A 3C 4B
3
1 get ... over with
2 smooth over
3 running over
4 passed over
4 1C 2A 3B

Revision exercises

1
1 take over
2 passed over
3 smooth over
4 get ... over with
5 put over
6 think over

UP

A Increasing and Improving Part 1

1 1D 2H 3B 4C 5G 6A 7F 8E
2
1 gone up
2 backed up
3 built up
4 cheer up
5 do up
6 dress up
7 bring up
8 brush up
3
1 doing up
2 brought up
3 gone up
4 brush up
5 backed up
6 build up
7 dressed up
8 Cheer up

A Increasing and Improving Part 2

1 1D 2E 3A 4G 5H 6B 7C 8F

2
1 Speed up
2 speak up
3 grew up
4 stir up
5 save up
6 push up
7 speak up
8 pick up
3
1 speak up
2 speed up
3 pick up
4 speak up
5 save up
6 pushing up
7 grew up
8 pick up

B Preparing

1
1 fix up
2 draw up
3 soften up
4 set up
2 1D 2A 3E 4C 5B
3
1 set up
2 fixed up
3 soften up
4 drawn up
5 warming up
4
1 set up
2 fix up
3 drawn up
4 warm up
5 softening up

C Approaching

1
1 face up to
2 lives up to
3 keep up
4 come up against
2 1D 2B 3A 4C 5E
3
1 lived up to
2 face up to
3 catch up with
4 comes up against
5 keep up
4
1 catching up, keeping up
2 come up against
3 living up to
4 face up to
5 keep up

D Disrupting and Damaging

1 1E 2C 3A 4B 5F 6D
2
1 blow up
2 mess up
3 held up
4 broke up
5 mixed up
6 slipped up

3
1 mess up
2 slipped up
3 blown up
4 breaking up
5 mix up
6 holding up
4 1B 2C 3A

E Completing and Finishing Part 1

1 1G 2F 3H 4C 5B 6A 7E 8D
2
1 clear up
2 do up
3 ended up
4 Drink up
5 checking up
6 followed up
7 clears up
8 cover up
3
1 followed up
2 ended up
3 did up
4 drank up
5 clears up
6 clear up
7 checking up
8 cover up

E Completing and Finishing Part 2

1 1D 2G 3C 4B 5F 6E 7A
2
1 tidying up
2 giving up
3 weigh up
4 summed up
5 pull up
6 wound up
7 use up
3
1 gave up
2 weighing up
3 wind up
4 use up
5 sum up
6 pull up
7 tidy up
4 1D 2C 3E 4B 5A

F Happening and Creating

1
1 pick up
2 bring up
3 come up with
4 think up
5 make up
2 1E 2F 3C 4A 5G 6B 7D 8H

3 1 brought up
2 come up
3 making up
4 pick up
5 picked up
6 come up with
7 turns up
8 thought up

4 1 come up, turned up
2 pick up
3 thought up
4 pick up
5 making up
6 bring up
7 turning up
8 come up with

G **Collecting and Being together**

1 1 look up
2 take ... up on
3 puts up
4 make up
5 pick up

2 1C 2D 3B 4E 5A

3 1 make up
2 put up
3 took ... up on
4 look up
5 pick up

4 1 made up
2 take ... up on
3 look up
4 put up
5 pick up

H **Other meanings**

1 1 make up for
2 look up
3 take up
4 turns up
5 put up with

2 1C 2A 3B 4D 5E

3 1 put up with
2 look up
3 took up
4 turn up
5 make up for

4 1D 2C 3B 4A

Revision exercise

1 1 broke up
2 make up
3 follow up
4 tidy up
5 bring up
6 clear up
7 doing up
8 face up to
9 gave up
10 come up
11 held up
12 backed up
13 do up
14 set up
15 put up with
16 mess up
17 built up
18 Look up
19 wound up
20 lived up to
21 pick up
22 save up
23 grow up
24 brushing up
25 Draw up
26 turned up
27 weigh up
28 keep up

OTHER PARTICLES

AHEAD

1 1 plan ahead
2 get ahead
3 lies ahead
4 go ahead

2 1B 2A 3D 4C

3 1 lay ahead
2 plan ahead
3 go ahead
4 get ahead

4 1 get ahead
2 plan ahead
3 lay ahead
4 going ahead

APART

1 1 tears apart
2 take apart
3 falls apart
4 take apart

2 1B 2A 3D 4C

3 1 taken apart
2 falling apart
3 torn apart
4 take apart

4 1 take apart
2 tearing apart
3 take apart
4 fall apart

AROUND/ROUND/ ABOUT

1 1 bring about
2 get around/round
3 stick around
4 get around/round to
5 bring around/round

2 1E 2D 3A 4B 5C

3 1 get around to
2 get round
3 bring round
4 brought about
5 stick around

4 1 stick around
2 bring about
3 get around/round
4 brought around/round
5 got around/round to

BY

1 1 get by
2 drop by
3 stand by
4 put by

2 1C 2A 3D 4B

3 1 put by
2 gets by
3 Drop by
4 stand by

4 1 get by
2 standing by
3 dropped by
4 put by

FORWARD

1 1 put forward
2 look forward to
3 bring forward, put forward
4 goes forward

2 1A 2C 3D 4B

3 1 put forward
2 go forward
3 look forward to
4 brought forward

4 1 goes forward
2 brought forward, put forward
3 put forward
4 look forward to, am looking forward to

THROUGH

1 1 put through
2 think through
3 falls through
4 go through with
5 pulls through

2 1D 2A 3E 4B 5C

3 1 put through
2 go through with
3 pull through
4 think through
5 fallen through

4 1 pulled through
2 go through with
3 fell through
4 thought through
5 putting through

TOGETHER

1 1 piece together
2 put together
3 pull together
4 get together

2 1C 2B 3D 4A

3 1 put together
2 piece together
3 Pull together
4 get together

4 1 get together
2 pull together
3 put together
4 piece together

Sample answer for exercise 4, page 11 (memorization paragraph):

I <u>got back</u> 7 days later on a wet, windy Wednesday. I phoned Felicity straight away as I had promised – I never <u>go back on</u> my promises. She wasn't in. She had gone to the zoo to <u>take</u> the seventh pink elephant <u>back</u>. I said I'd <u>call back</u> at 7. Why was she <u>giving</u> the elephant <u>back</u>? I went <u>back over</u> the elephant-napping in my mind. The only answer was that the seventh pink elephant had <u>bounced back</u> to health. Felicity must have <u>fallen back on</u> Plan B.